THE LIONEL LEGEND

ROBERT SCHLEICHER

Voyageur Press

First published in 2008 by MBI Publishing Company and Voyageur Press, an imprint of MBI Publishing Company, 400 First Avenue North, Suite 300, Minneapolis, MN 55401 USA

Voyageur Press titles are also available at discounts in bulk quantity for industrial or sales-promotional use. For details write to Special Sales Manager at MBI Publishing Company, 400 First Avenue North, Suite 300, Minneapolis, MN 55401 USA.

To find out more about our books, join us online at www.voyageurpress.com.

Library of Congress
Cataloging-in-Publication Data

Schleicher, Robert.
  The Lionel legend : an american icon / By Robert Schleicher.
    p. cm.
  ISBN 978-0-7603-3482-9 (hb w/ jkt)
  1. Cowen, Joshua Lionel, 1880-1965. 2. Lionel Corporation—Biography. 3. Railroads—Models—History. I. Title.
  TF140.C65S34 2008
  625.1'9—dc22
                          2008032749

On the title pages
A re-creation of the famous scene from the cover of the 1947 Lionel catalog, with a full-scale Harriman 2-8-0 (in place of Pennsylvania Railroad 2-6-2) thundering past the Automatic Gateman's shed.

Editor: Leah Noel
Designer: Sara Holle
Jacket designer: John Barnett

Printed in the United States of America

CONTENTS

PART I

LIONEL: AN AMERICAN LEGEND

L ionel trains, along with their orange and blue logos, are longtime American icons. No one needs to say "toy train" when talking about Lionel, because for generations of Americans, Lionel is and was all about toy trains. Lionel trains are legendary—an important part of America's history and the legacy of finding a toy train set under the Christmas tree.

Lionel trains have been around for just over a century, long enough so that nearly everyone's grandfather had a Lionel train set or wanted one. Today, when probably three-fourths of the population has never traveled by train, even a commuter train, the excitement behind these toys and trains in general might seem a mystery. You may just need to see one in action to understand how fascinating trains are. There is something magical about a hundred cars following and flowing perfectly behind one another, especially through a series of curves. Get up close and you can live to tell about how an earthquake feels. And the sound! The deafening clatter of a full hundred tons of metal trying to shake its way free from the steel rails as each car flashes by is overwhelming. Romantic, perhaps, but also terrifying to think about how much havoc this monster would create if it derailed.

Today, Thomas the Tank, the *Hogwarts Express*, and *The Polar Express* delight yet another generation—and you can put any of these in the hands of an eight-year-old thanks to Lionel's reproductions. Lionel's legacy lives on, still fulfilling children's dreams year after year after year, generation after generation after generation. Even when those children grow up and have children or even grandchildren of their own, they can share in their love of Lionel trains. Yes, you can run Lionel's newest *Hogwarts Express* on the same track that the 1936 Lionel *Blue Comet* traveled on or put that classic *Blue Comet* on a modern Lionel FasTrack layout.

THE ROMANCE OF THE RAILS, AT HOME

It might be difficult to create a toy that would talk like Thomas, transport you to Hogwarts School of Witchcraft and Wizardry, or carry you to the North Pole, but Lionel's replicas come very close. To a child, these toy trains are massive, their rumble thundering. They even have a whistle, giving them that extra boost of authenticity.

For an older generation, travel by train was something to dream about. The *Zephyr, 20th Century Limited, City of San Francisco, Broadway Limited, Southern Crescent,* and *Empire Builder* were the magic carpets to far-off lands. And for most people in the 1930s, 1940s, and 1950s, the likelihood of travel by carpet was about as great as the likelihood of travel by train. But you could bring those dreams into your home by running Lionel's re-creation of the *20th Century Limited* or *Broadway Limited* right across your living room or basement floor.

LIVING LIONEL

Lionel sparked dreams by becoming very effective at marketing its products. It offered tantalizing catalog deals, along with photos of how to make your own train set a magical wonderland. In the 1940s, Lionel knew that a lot of returning soldiers had become fathers right after World War II, and they were

Magazine ads like this one for the 1954 Lionel catalog helped sell Lionel to the fathers of the baby boom generation. When their children looked inside the catalog, they saw the bold new models of the Katy Railroad's *Texas Special* passenger train, an all-new replica of the Fairbanks-Morse giant Trainmaster freight diesel, an operating rotary beacon, a switch tower where one man comes out the door and another climbs the stairs, a magnetic crane, and a station that automatically starts and stops the train.

Opposite page: For many Lionel fans, the most significant Lionel locomotives were the company's replicas of the ElectroMotive Corporation's F3A and F3B diesels, like Bill Hitchcock's New York Central and Santa Fe locomotives from 1948.

looking for ways to connect with their children. Television still being a new thing, Lionel used magazine ads in the *Saturday Evening Post, Newsweek,* and other periodicals to speak directly to dads.

The ad promoting the 1954 Lionel catalog touted that the 44-page product listing was full of color photography (at a time when even *Life* magazine was mostly black and white), and by ordering it, you'd also receive a 78-rpm record of bells,

Peter Perry's layout is comprised of Lionel FasTrack, and he operates newer Lionel equipment beside the lithographed stamped-steel buildings and tunnels from Lionel's 1930s tin era.

Right: Michael Sadowski's 20x20-foot Lionel layout utilizes 72-inch curves and turnouts so that he can operate the largest locomotives and longest cars anywhere on the layout.

whistles, and railroad sound effects and Lionel's special "Pop Persuader" card to convince Dad to buy a Lionel train set by listing all the reasons why life could simply not go on without one.

CREATE YOUR OWN WORLD

At the same time, Lionel's catalogs, box art, and advertisements clearly illustrated that you could create your own world on the floor or, better, a tabletop. Before nearly every product came prefabricated, people prided themselves in being able to put things together themselves. Lionel made the railroad part simple. If you were a little bit of an artist and if you could actually plaster a wall (a common skill of many homeowners in the 1940s and 1950s), you could complete the hills and mountains and valleys for a fully scenic Lionel layout like those shown in Lionel's catalog and in Lionel's own consumer magazine *Model*

Builder. Again, modern hobby materials such as plaster cloth and ground-colored foam make it even easier and quicker to create vast scenic vistas.

ACTION ACCESSORIES

Lionel brought a different kind of realism to the tabletop (or floor) with accessories that had action beyond that of the moving trains. Train set signals turned red when the adjacent track was occupied by a train, railroad signalmen moved out of their gatehouse to wave a lantern when the train passed, and freight cars could be unloaded by remote control. Lionel's log loaders, coal loaders, magnetic cranes, barrel loaders, and a host of others, all loaded or unloaded by remote control.

In the 1940s, the buildings on most Lionel layouts were cardboard. Virtually none were plastic, and metal was scarce (after all, there had just been a metal-consuming war). So cardboard,

Left: Floor-to-ceiling scenery, like this canyon on Oliver Gaddini's layout, is possible with easy-to-use plaster cloth.

Below: Les Kushner assembled these structures from Ameri-Towne-brand plastic modular wall components on this 4x8-foot FasTrack layout.

colored and die-cut, was used in kits that built entire cities, railroad stations, castles, farms, and bridges. Lionel offered several such cardboard models as part of its annual "catalog package" deals. During World War II, when there were no Lionel trains, Lionel even offered die-cut cardboard trains to get you through the war years. Today, with plastic kits full of ready-built buildings, you can build a complete train city in less than a week.

TRAIN TECHNOLOGY

As for trains, Lionel produced "tinplates" before World War II. With the exception of the wheels, axles, and other shafts, nearly every component on Lionel's locomotives, cars, accessories, and track at that time was made of stamped steel in this era because die-casting production was still too expensive for toy trains. Yet while made of steel, the locomotives and cars were often plated with tin to prevent rust (which is why the tinplate name surfaced and stuck).

Five trains can operate simultaneously on the three-level FasTrack layout built by Les Kushner of Main Line Hobbies in East Norriton, Pennsylvania.

Right: One of Lionel's first post–World War II locomotives was this replica of the Pennsylvania Railroad's unique 6-8-6 steam turbine that was still running in 1948.

Lionel began to change its production methods in the early 1940s, from using nearly all stamped metal to construct its train to using die-cast zinc. The die-casting machinery was needed during World War II, when Lionel factories were converted to manufacture components such as compasses for ships and war machinery. So Lionel's 1938 die-cast metal replica of the New York Central 4-6-4 Hudson was the most realistic and rugged model of that train made until the 1950s. Lionel also produced similarly detailed cast-metal freight cars and a 0-6-0 steam locomotive before World War II.

Soon after the war ended, Lionel introduced an all-new die-cast replica of the Pennsylvania Railroad's very unusual steam turbine 6-8-6 locomotive, as well as a line of plastic-bodied cars. Today, Lionel is still making die-cast trains and cars, but ones designed in the United States and produced in China. Lionel also offers exact-scale replicas of some of the largest locomotives out there, such as the modern-era EMD SD70MAC diesel and the 1940s-era Union Pacific 4-8-8-4 Big Boy steam locomotive.

By 1954, Lionel locomotives were usually equipped with magnetic locomotive wheels for more traction on steel rails

(Lionel called it Magne-Traction), as well as simulated steam locomotive whistles or diesel horns—digitally recorded sound was over a half-century in the future (unless, of course, you had that 78-rpm record).

LIONEL LIVES ON . . . BARELY

Lionel's sales peaked at about $33 million in 1954 and declined steadily through 1950s to less than $15 million in 1958, with nearly a decade of earning no profit for their shareholders.

For many of those who grew up between the 1950s and 1990s, HO scale toy trains were the only trains they knew. So many later-born baby boomers missed the chance to experience the magic of Lionel because Lionel had almost disappeared. Interest in real trains was diminishing about the same time that truly inexpensive toy trains became available at every toy store, department store, and in the new discount stores. Those trains were half the size of a Lionel train and about a tenth of the price. It's no surprise the smaller HO trains easily outsold Lionel. Lionel even offered a few HO locomotives, cars, and train sets, but it was a half-hearted effort that was, most often, just a repackage or a reproduction of another toy train brand, Athearn.

Athearn was the king of HO trains in the 1950s and 1960s, but the brand did not create the nostalgia behind it that Lionel has. In fact, every year you'll find Christmas ornaments, lamps, clocks, clothing, and a host of other items with the Lionel brand logo on it, and virtually nothing with Athearn's or American Flyer's (Lionel's competitor in the 1940s and 1950s).

Nevertheless, the popularity of HO trains nearly drove Lionel out of business in the 1960s. To save the brand, the corporation leased its name rights and tooling in 1969 to cereal maker General Mills for further use. General Mills produced the trains under its Fundimensions division and gradually rebuilt Lionel's all-but-lost reputation for quality and service.

One of Lionel's longtime fans, Richard Kughn, organized a company to purchase Lionel in 1985, and he further rebuilt the company in the ensuing years. Since then, Lionel has remained the largest model train company in America.

YOU CAN COUNT ON LIONEL

Few consumer products have maintained their image of quality for as long as Lionel trains. Lionel certainly had dark periods when its trains weren't the best, but today's Lionel is truly better than ever. It is much easier to get a Lionel train

set operating than virtually any other, and it will continue to run for years and years.

From the get-go, Lionel created a product that worked the first time. The track was sturdy enough to walk on, and the locomotives were powerful and reliable. Yes, you did have to clean the oxidation from the track and wheels, but for those accustomed to changing a screw-in fuse in the home circuit box, this type of maintenance was easy. In the last decade of the century, the term "plug and play" became used to describe toys that required little assembly. Lionel has always been one of these. You really could assemble the most complex Lionel model railroad, with hundreds of feet of track and dozens of switches, in a weekend.

A few years ago, Lionel improved upon the steel track it had been producing for a century with FasTrack, a much more realistic track with simulated loose rock ballast, scale-size ties, and a less obtrusive center third rail. Today, FasTrack makes it even easier and quicker to assemble a Lionel layout.

Lionel has always had a policy that today's train should be completely compatible with yesterday's. If the models were designed to run O Gauge three-rail track, you could still operate a 1930 Lionel New York Central electric locomotive on Lionel's 2008 FasTrack.

The Lionel legend is portrayed on these pages, from Lionel's massive Standard Gauge toy trains of the 1920s to the exact-scale replicas of today's diesels. This book is not intended to be a catalog; it would take six books this size to illustrate all the items Lionel has created. The Lionel products you see on these pages are, to me, the ones that were most significant in the 100-years-and-counting that established Lionel as an American legend.

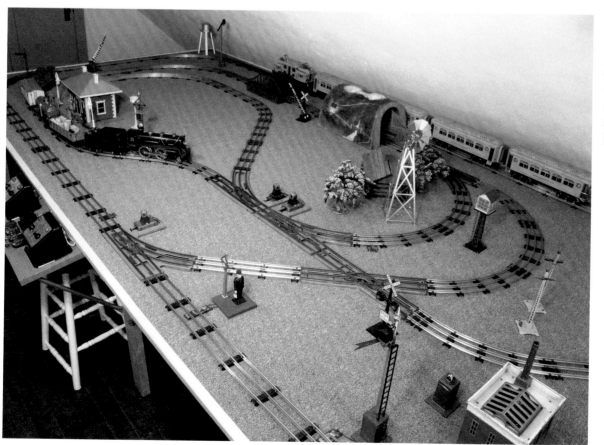

Ken Huber's Standard Gauge layout is assembled entirely from Lionel's massive stamped-tin cars, locomotives, structures, and bridges from the 1930s.

Lionel's railroad action goes beyond rails to include machines that collect logs dumped by an Operating Log Car and then load them onto another waiting car. Lionel offered similar action with coal, barrels culverts, and cartons like this string of remote-control accessories on Oliver Gaddini's layout.

A POSITIVE SPIN

Lionel was the most active of all the toy companies in getting the message to moms and dads that this was the one toy necessary for any child. Lionel was one of the pioneers in public relations and product placement, getting the Lionel train image in front of many millions and as often as possible.

In the era before the interstates and prior to jet passenger travel, America was focused on train travel. Virtually every talk show in the 1940s and 1950s had a railroad enthusiast as a featured guest, and many of them wanted to show off their Lionel layouts. Lionel trains appeared on the covers of the *Saturday Evening Post* and most of the other weekly magazines, with "train photo ops" with dignitaries as diverse as Pope Pius XII and baseball legends Joe DiMaggio and Roy Campanella.

Today, singer Neil Young helps with Lionel's development of the TrainMaster and Lionel Legacy electronic control systems.

Lionel's major marketing success, however, was getting its trains into the windows of department stores across America. Lionel's marketing folks worked closely with some of the stores to get the trains placed there in the 1940s and 1950s. Other stores knew that trains were at least as important as Christmas trees in getting customers' attention. And, in the first half of the twentieth century, trains were one of the few "action" items available to draw customers' attention.

Lionel provided some of the first point-of-purchase displays and introduced marketing that would become common for soap and cereal but was unusual in the world of toys. Lionel

Lionel's 1948 catalog offer included a set of six cutout cardboard buildings and, the rage of the day, 3-D blue-and-red photographs that could be viewed through the included pair of cardboard and plastic Stereopticon Eyeglasses—all for just a quarter.

The United States was at war in 1941, and Lionel proudly proclaimed it was producing "precision instruments for the United States Navy" on the cover of its catalog while using detailed drawings to introduce its action accessories, like the coal elevator, log loader, magnetic crane, and bascule bridge.

NEW, 1941 COLOR CATALOG

★ Sixty-four pages thick and printed in full colors, the new, 1941 Lionel catalog pictures the greatest fleet of trains Lionel has ever rolled out on the rails. New, low, long, highly realistic "O" gauge passenger cars. New, low-price, scale-detailed freight cars. New colors, new combinations, a spectacu-

lar new line... once for yo... log and ge... delay. Use... go to you... ware or e... Lionel cat...

DON'T WAIT! CLIP AND MAIL THIS COUPON AT ONCE

LIONEL Dept. M, 15 East 26th...
Enclosed is 10 cents...
copy of new Lionel Catalog...

Name————
Address————
City————

NOVEMBER 1941

Happiest Christmas Dream in any Boy's life... LIONEL TRAINS!

When a boy dreams about getting trains, he dreams about Lionel Trains. A bright and shining dream that's alive with flashing action and the click of rails and the deep whistle of smoke-puffing engines. Why it's half the fun of being a boy!

That's been a Christmas dream of adventure, fun and thrills that Lionel has been a part of for over 50 years. And today the name Lionel stands for the most famous trains, the most wanted trains in the whole wide world of boys. Take him with you to a Lionel Dealer.. let him see all the wonderful Lionel trains in action.

Only LIONEL TRAINS can match your boy's dream...the world's leaders. Only LIONEL TRAINS are built with real R.R. Knuckle Couplers, Die-Cast Trucks and Solid Steel Wheels in addition to realistic puffing smoke and built-in two-tone whistle.

GET A REAL ENGINEER'S CAP LIKE THIS FOR YOUR BOY! See Extra-Special Coupon Offer Below

EXTRA-SPECIAL COUPON OFFER!
ALL for 50¢

Official Engineer's Cap, in striped denim, plus 5 R.R. insignia emblems to wear on it, together with Catalog, Rule Book and Building Kit, all for only 50¢.
✓Check Cap Size here
SMALL | MEDIUM | LARGE

LIONEL TRAINS, P. O. Box 9, Dept. EEE, New York 46, N. Y.

TWO OFFERS CHECK ONE

☐ I enclose 25¢ for catalog offer below—
1. The new 36-page full color Lionel catalog.
2. Rule Book (including signals) for Model Railroaders.
3. Model R.R. Town Building Kit—Stores, etc.
OR
☐ I enclose 50¢ for catalog offer above plus engineer's cap.

Name————
Address————
City————
Zone———— State————

Mention the National Geographic—It identifies you

The advertisements for the 1952 Lionel catalog included a 25-cent package deal that included the catalog; a book of condensed, real railroad rules; and a full-color set of cutout town buildings. For 50 cents more, you could get an official engineer's cap.

Lionel played its nostalgia card with the 1950s-era products and look that were featured in this 1999 ad.

also trained its salespeople well, and the salespeople, in turn, trained the clerks who would come face to face with customers in the department stores.

Lionel's own New York City showroom was located at 15 East 29th Street in 1926, and it featured a massive layout that visitors could control from an elevated signal tower. Lionel's marketing folks made certain that stories about that showroom layout appeared in every weekly news magazine in America, especially near the Christmas holidays.

Lionel was arguably more effective at conveying the image of a father bonding with his son over trains than Daisy was in marketing its air rifles. You just knew you could get closer to Dad if you showed him the ad (assuming he did not already see it in *Popular Mechanics* or some other magazine), and you knew it would help your case to see other dads and kids playing with their Lionel trains. Plus, Lionel trains had the advantage

of winning Mom over because you wouldn't "put an eye out" with a Lionel train.

Boys have always been fascinated by contests, and Lionel had several of them, ranging from providing photos of your layout for prizes to publishing those layouts in Lionel's *Model Builder* magazine during the 1930s and 1940s, to promoting its RailScope onboard video camera by showing some of the videos from customer's trains in the 1980s.

In the 1990s, Thomas the Tank Engine became a popular children's television show character, and Lionel partnered with the creators to produce Thomas the Tank trains, helping to introduce Lionel to yet another generation of kids. Then *The Polar Express* movie debuted in 2005 and the wildly popular Harry Potter series featured the *Hogwarts Express*, giving more children a chance to fall in love with trains. Lionel has them all, ready to run around your layout.

LIONEL'S LIBRARY

Setting up a Lionel train and track certainly takes some assembly, but once you've pushed enough track sections together to make an oval, screwed on the wires (assuming you knew how to strip the insulation from the wires), and plugged in the transformer, you're ready to go. The next step, building an entire city or countryside, certainly takes more skill and vast amounts of imagination, and it is part of the reason Lionel realized it needed to provide instructions beyond what was furnished with each switch, turnout, or signal.

First, Lionel published its own consumer magazine, *Model Builder*, which featured not only simple but realistic small layouts but also 40x80-foot club layouts to inspire railfans' personal setups. Then Lionel realized model railroaders wanted a permanent reference book to better illustrate both the dream of a complete model railroad and the seemingly simple steps to create such an empire.

Lionel already had the material from the *Model Builder* magazines, so in 1940, Lionel published the first edition of the 192-page *Handbook for Model Builders*. It might seem like a long way from playing with toy trains, but you really did need to have model-building skills if you wanted a ballasted track, a complex signal system, hills and valleys, a river and

bridges, and buildings of all kinds. I can credit the inspiration for my career as an author of model railroad books to my first copy of the *Handbook for Model Builders*. (I made an even swap with an older—and presumably wiser—neighbor, trading my O-27 Lionel 6-8-6 steam turbine locomotive for the book plus a well-crashed O-27 *Zephyr* and two metal coaches. Dollarwise, I probably lost out by at least 100 percent, but it spawned a career.)

Lionel went back into the book business in 1950, but this time partnering with Pocketbooks, who published and distributed Lionel's new book, *Model Railroading*, which ended up on most newsstands in America. The first edition of the 4⅛x6¼-inch paperback had 256 black and white pages, but by the printing of the sixth edition in 1961, the book had grown to 384 pages.

I was doing consulting and public relations work for the MPC division of Fundimensions in the 1980s, and I knew needed a more up-to-date book for Lionel fans. Finally, in 1986, the company agreed, and I created *The Lionel Train Book* with 132 pages to bring the information on how to get more enjoyment from Lionel trains up to date. It stayed in print for nearly 20 years.

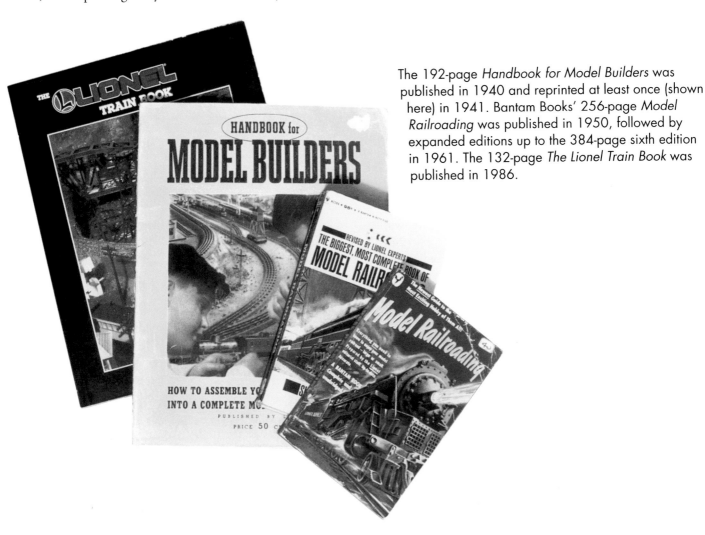

The 192-page *Handbook for Model Builders* was published in 1940 and reprinted at least once (shown here) in 1941. Bantam Books' 256-page *Model Railroading* was published in 1950, followed by expanded editions up to the 384-page sixth edition in 1961. The 132-page *The Lionel Train Book* was published in 1986.

Lionel advertised the *Handbook for Model Builders* in a hardback version in the February 1943 issue of *Model Builder* magazine.

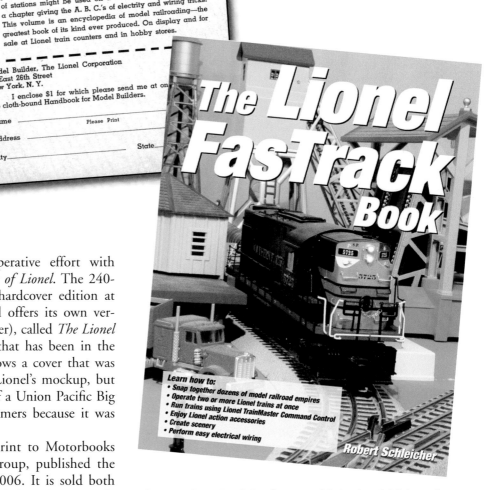

Learn how to:
- Snap together dozens of model railroad empires
- Operate two or more Lionel trains at once
- Run trains using Lionel TrainMaster Command Control
- Enjoy Lionel action accessories
- Create scenery
- Perform easy electrical wiring

Robert Schleicher

In 2004, Lionel agreed to a cooperative effort with Motorbooks to publish the *The Big Book of Lionel*. The 240-page softcover book also was sold as a hardcover edition at Barnes & Noble for a while, and Lionel offers its own version of the book (featuring a different cover), called *The Lionel Train Book*. And *The Lionel Train Book* that has been in the Lionel catalogs for the past five years shows a cover that was never published—that cover photo was Lionel's mockup, but the company decided on using a photo of a Union Pacific Big Boy with operating buttons and transformers because it was more typical of Lionel layout.

Finally, Voyageur Press, a sister imprint to Motorbooks and part of the Quayside Publishing Group, published the 160-page *The Lionel FasTrack Book* in 2006. It is sold both through book dealers and through Lionel, but there is only one version. Each printing, however, has been updated slightly to add new part numbers.

The Lionel FasTrack Book was published in 2006, and virtually identical editions are available from Lionel and bookstores.

The Big Book of Lionel was published in 2004 in both a paperback edition and in hardcover that was only sold through the Barnes & Noble bookstore chain.

The Lionel catalogs from 2004 until today offer The Lionel Train Book, but the cover in the Lionel catalogs is not correct—this is the only cover used on that book.

LIONEL'S MAGAZINES

Lionel effectively created the market for toy trains though every conceivable marketing effort. Boys read comic books profusely in the 1930s and 1940s, the main reason Lionel used a full-color comic-book-style cover for many of the issues of its own newsstand magazine, *Model Builder*.

Lionel has long offered magazines with content that included much more than just longer descriptions of current locomotives, cars, accessories, or sets. The company's early magazines included how-to articles, photos of readers' layouts, track plans, and letters-to-the-editor columns. From 1930 to 1936, Lionel's magazine was titled *The Lionel Magazine: The Model Railroad Magazine for Every Boy*, and it was published quarterly at first and eventually came out 10 times a year. In 1937, Lionel introduced *Model Builder* magazine, which was published until 1946, usually at the rate of six issues a year. The predecessor to *Model Builder* was *Model Engineer*, which appeared only for a November/December 1936 issue. Lionel discovered there already was a British magazine with that title, thus the reason for the name change.

Model Builder was always a product of its time. During World War II, the magazine had to cut back on the number of pages, and it adopted three-color covers, usually simplified drawings of real railroad scenes. Lionel was not allowed to produce toy trains during the war, so *Model Builder* was the company's only hope of keeping its customers' interests alive. In 1944, with the war coming to an end, Lionel used photographs of model railroads on the cover.

Then in September 1946, the magazine became a 9x12-inch size, but to keep costs down, the covers were photos supplied by real railroad companies. The magazine usually included advertisements from larger dealers, as well as toolmakers and structure and accessory manufacturers. The magazine's circulation seems to have held relatively steady at around 30,000 to 40,000 copies, but no official records were kept. Even though enthusiasts were familiar with it, clearly only a small fraction of Lionel's hundreds of thousands of fans cared enough about their toys to invest in a magazine when they could use at least part of the money to buy more track or switches or cars.

In 1976, Lionel introduced its *Keep On Trackin'* magazine, available only to members of Lionel Railroader Club. The title was changed to *The Lionel Railroader Club* for one issue in 1982, with a contest for readers to rename the publication.

From 1982 until today, the publication has been called *Inside Track*. Most of the issues from 1970s, 1980s, and 1990s were just two- or three-color but, more recently, the publication has been four-color with an average of about 16 pages per issue. It is generally published quarterly as part of membership in the Lionel Railroader Club (www.lionel.com). The articles focus on highlighting features of new locomotives and cars, reader's letters, and offers for special Lionel Railroader Club products.

Lionel advertised the new *Model Builder* magazine in its 1937 catalog.

The late-1930s issues of *Model Builder* often featured a photo of a dad and son at work on their Lionel locomotive or layout.

In 1939, Lionel advertised this spectacular Locoscope to convince newsstand customers to subscribe to *Model Builder* magazine.

In the early 1940s, the covers of *Model Builder* used lower-cost line-art illustrations.

MODEL BUILDER

MARCH, 1944

10¢

INSIDE TRACK

OFFICIAL PUBLICATION OF THE LIONEL RAILROADER CLUB SUMMER 2007 ISSUE 117

Southern Pacific 4436 Class GS-4 Daylight
The Most Beautiful Trains in the World

Milwaukee Road Class EP-2 Bipolar Electrics
The Mightiest Electric Locomotives in the World

LIONEL RAILROADER CLUB

Today, Lionel publishes the quarterly *Inside Track* magazine for members of the Lionel Railroader Club.

LIONEL'S CATALOG DREAMS

Lionel knew from the company's first days that it had to sell a dream, not just a train set. It did that mostly through its catalogs, in which Lionel's artists created an entire world within the pages. Romantic images of trains rushing across the pages into some imaginary but distant destination were common, and so were themes where all of the goods from the entire world could be delivered to you and by you with your Lionel train. With one look at the Lionel catalog, you were certain all that could happen, here and now.

Lionel's first catalogs in 1902 were black and white, illustrated primarily with line art, as were most magazines of the period. Lionel offered two-color catalogs as early as 1913, and by 1921, the catalogs had started to use four-color photography. Through the 1930s, the catalog covers were usually paintings of a boy and his dad (or a real railroad engineer) and their Lionel trains. The illustrations inside were typical of the period, with heavily retouched color photographs.

Lionel's catalogs in the 1940s and 1950s were illustrated exclusively with paintings of the products. The artist could tone down the oversize rails and 10-foot gaps between the cars and the toylike proportions to make the Lionel trains look far more realistic than they were (or are, for that matter). Surprisingly, no one noticed that the proportions of the actual Lionel models were not really those of the catalogs. In fact, few modeling enthusiasts felt that miniature trains should be completely accurate, with correct-size rails (and just two—not three—of them), and that helped spawn the model railroad hobby, particularly the HO scale version of it.

Lionel's image was altered from a dream to photo reality in the late 1950s, when the catalogs used unretouched color photographs of Lionel trains. These types of photographs were used until the late 1990s, when a few catalogs were illustrated with evocative and stylish paintings. By 2000, Lionel reverted to using color photographs again, but by

Lionel's 1937 catalog cover featured its new exact-scale New York Central 4-6-4 Hudson.

then the company's Standard O trains were as realistic as any you could buy.

Most Lionel enthusiasts have their personal favorite catalog, the one that provided the spark that ignited their lifelong passion for Lionel. In fact, bound versions of reprinted Lionel catalogs have been available so that enthusiasts could purchase their favorites again. Some of the milestone Lionel catalogs that are among my favorites are the 1940 catalog, the 1946 catalog, and the 1958 catalog. The 1940 catalog illustrated Lionel at its prewar best with historical stamped-steel Standard Gauge and the newest exact-scale Hudson and freight cars. The 1946 catalog marked the true end of World War II for many and featured Lionel's first mass-produced highly detailed plastic models, while the 1958 catalog was the space age edition with rockets and radar on the cover and the associated products inside.

In 1990, Lionel's catalog proved the company was back on track with some of the first precisely detailed products that were to become staples for the next decade and more. The 1996 catalog was really a work of art with incredible paintings on every page. The 2000 catalog was a fitting tribute to Lionel's 100th anniversary, with a range of products as vast as that 1940 catalog.

Lionel's first postwar catalog in 1946 featured the all-new Pennsylvania 6-8-6 steam turbine.

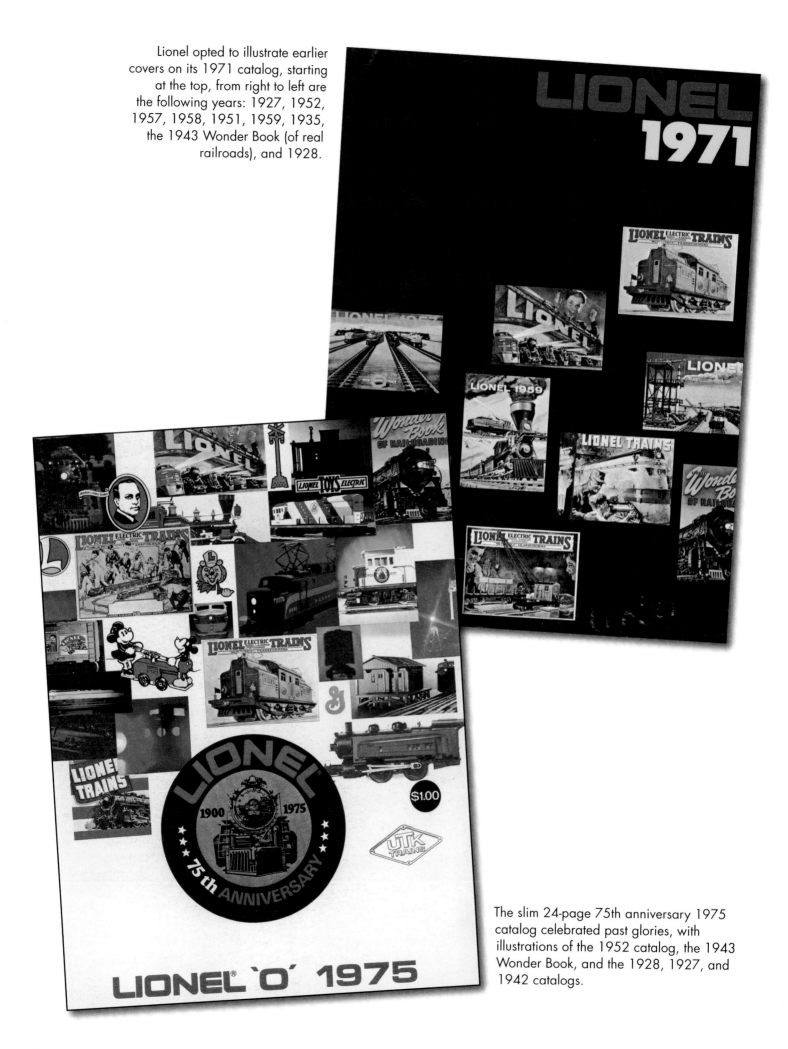

Lionel opted to illustrate earlier covers on its 1971 catalog, starting at the top, from right to left are the following years: 1927, 1952, 1957, 1958, 1951, 1959, 1935, the 1943 Wonder Book (of real railroads), and 1928.

The slim 24-page 75th anniversary 1975 catalog celebrated past glories, with illustrations of the 1952 catalog, the 1943 Wonder Book, and the 1928, 1927, and 1942 catalogs.

The exact-scale New York Central Hudson graced Lionel's 100th anniversary catalog in 2000.

Lionel's scale replica of the Milwaukee Road's Bipolar electric locomotive was featured on the cover of the 218-page Volume I 2007 catalog.

ENSURING LIONEL'S QUALITY

Over the years, Lionel has built a reputation of producing models that are reliable and, if a mechanical problem does develop, Lionel has always provided the necessary fix. In the 1940s and 1950s, Lionel tested every locomotive and every accessory to be sure it operated properly before putting it into the box. As production techniques were developed, Lionel tested only a few samples of each product. That worked fairly well until the 1960s, when machines and assembly jigs began to wear and lower-quality materials were used to help lower prices.

However, Lionel survived this dent in its image because of its authorized Lionel repair stations. In the 1930s and 1940s, Lionel established its better dealers as Authorized Service Stations. With special tools and testing devices, these service stations had the capacity to repair any locomotive, car, accessory, or switch. Lionel also trained the dealer's servicemen and supplied nearly every part to the service stations. Lionel still maintains a network of these Authorized Service Stations, although much of today's repairs require complete component replacement rather than repair.

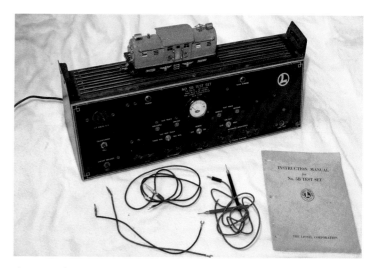

The Lionel 5B Test Set was nearly three-feet long with five rails to accommodate O, OO, and Standard Gauge locomotives. It had meters and cables to check transformers, locomotives, whistle tenders, and accessories. This one is in Chris Gans' collection at Nicholas Smith Trains in Broomall, Pennsylvania.

Today, a Lionel Authorized Service Station would simply replace a complete wheel and gear assembly, but in the 1930s and 1940s the serviceman would use this No. ST301 Puller (bottom) to remove one wheel and the damaged gear to replace the gear with a new one. The wooden rack is the ST350-6 Tool Block, which includes all the rivet headers and punches needed to disassemble and re-rivet any Lionel model. These are used daily by Chuck Sartor at Mizell Trains in Westminster, Colorado.

Lionel offered comprehensive consumer manuals for operating and wiring the most complex Lionel layout.

The dark period in Lionel's reputation for quality control coincided with the dark ages for American automakers, when domestic manufacturers forgot about the importance of service after the sale. Today, quality control is a given for consumers, and it has become the controller of the marketplace—if the train doesn't run (yes, even if the buyer did not bother to plug the transformer into wall), the buyer will take it back to the store and expect an immediate and full refund. When the large chain stores buy a product, they insist that part of the contract with their supplier includes the guarantee that the manufacturer will replace any item the customer feels is faulty—the store does not have to bother to ask why, which is why many faulty products end up being discontinued.

PART II

TINPLATE TRAINS: THEN AND NOW

HEAR THE WHISTLE BLOW

Lionel's current steam locomotives use digitally recorded RailSounds whistles and other sounds like those inside this massive Union Pacific 4-12-2.

The phrase "hear the whistle blow" has lost its meaning in modern America. During the first three-quarters of the twentieth century, however, the whistle heralded the coming of the train, and that meant a young boy or girl often was waiting at the railroad crossing or station platform to see it pass by. The sound of a steam locomotive whistle was far more impressive than that of a modern diesel horn. Somehow, the whistle seemed to enter your consciousness through your solar plexus as much as through your ears.

The steam locomotive whistle was a late arrival in the Lionel line. Lionel had been shipping steam locomotives for nearly 30 years when, in 1935, it offered "a real whistle by Lionel." However, this whistle was not inside the locomotive, but inside a lithographed and stamped-tin station, No. 48W. It also was not a miniature recording, which were not available at the time. Instead, Lionel had devised a method of actually blowing air through a real whistle.

Lionel came up with the sound by first recording the actual whistles of nearby Lehigh Valley steam locomotives and matching the pitch and tone as closely as possible in its whistles. To make the air push through the in-the-tender whistle, Lionel installed a small motor and fan as part of the device. A button provided a small charge of DC current to activate the fan. Since the train was operated by AC current, the short bursts of DC did no harm other than to slightly slow the train. The enthusiast engineer could at long last blow the whistle to his or her heart's content.

Lionel included an instruction sheet with a listing of the short-long series of blasts that were the code that real engineers used to signal the crew to apply brakes, stop, and, of course, warn motorists and pedestrians and bicyclists at grade crossings.

Lionel's steam locomotives, like this 1948 No. 2026 2-6-2 on Bill Hitchcock's layout, were equipped with both smoke and motor-driven whistles (in the tenders) from the 1940s.

LIONEL TRAIN SETS

Ken Huber's Lionel Standard Gauge passenger set includes a No. 408E Engine, a No. 419 Combination Car, a No. 418 Pullman Car, a No. 431 Diner Car, and a No. 490 Observation Car from the mid-1930s.

The locomotive is what grabs your attention on both a real railroad and on a miniature railroad, and with good reason. The power that pulls that train is concentrated right there at the front. You cannot, however, operate a locomotive without track and a transformer to control it. And the locomotive looks lonely without at least a few cars to pull. So what you really need to get started with the hobby of model railroading (or the pastime of playing with toy trains) is everything in one box. Hence, the train set.

Lionel offered train sets in its earliest years, and over the decades it produced a train set to suit every market segment. You now can buy a $200 set at a big-box store or a $3,000 set at your local Lionel dealer. Obviously, the lower-priced sets are designed (and marketed) as entry-level products to make it as painless as possible for parents to get their kids started in the hobby.

This New York Central four-car train set on Gil Bruck's layout is from page 8 of the Lionel 2003 Volume 2 catalog. The New York Central *Limited* (with RailSounds) set includes Lionel's small replica of the EMD FT diesel and three cars.

Bill Hitchcock has collected examples of virtually every locomotive and car needed to re-create the train sets in Lionel's post–World War II catalogs. This is Lionel's No. 1464W Diesel 3-Car Pullman (plus a car) right off of page 12 of the 1951 catalog, with a pair of Alco FA-2 diesels and the silver smooth-side cars.

The year 1950 was a watershed one for Lionel train sets, when a large number of sets were offered. Gene Szymanowski used page 20 in Lionel's 1950 catalog as inspiration for this train that consists of a No. 671 Lionel 6-8-6 Steam Turbine with No. 671 Tender from 1946 to 1949 and Lionel Nos. 2421, 2422, 2423, and 2429 silver roof Pullman coaches from 1950 to 1953.

STANDARD GAUGE

In the early 1800s, America's railroads operated on a variety of different-sized track systems. The problems with moving freight and transporting soldiers during the Civil War made it clear a standard gauge (the distance between the tops of the railheads) track was needed. (Otherwise, freight or passengers had to be unloaded from one car and reloaded into another every time a different railroad was involved in their journey.) The railroads in America and most of the rest of world adopted track that was 4 feet wide and 8½ inches thick.

To a toy train fan, the term "standard gauge" means something completely different. Standard Gauge was the most common toy track gauge in the early part of the 1900s, with the biggest and best toy trains built to run on track with a 1¾-inch spacing between the railheads. By the 1920s, however, smaller and less expensive trains were produced to run on O Gauge (a term coined by British modelers) track with a distance of 1¼ inches between the railheads.

The earliest Lionel trains from 1901 to 1905 were actually re-creations of existing four-wheel trolleys and a small four-wheel electric switching locomotive that ran on massive track with rails spaced 2⅞ inches apart. Standard Gauge Lionel trains, with the rails spaced 1¾ inches apart, were introduced in 1906 and produced until the beginning of World War II. No exact scale was suggested for these toys but, based on the track gauge, they are about ⅟₃₂ scale. Lionel again produced trains to run on 1¾-inch gauge track in 1987 when the company began to produce large-scale trains to operate on what model railroaders call G Gauge track.

I have referred to the size of these toy trains by their track gauge. There is, however, another designation for toy and model trains known as scale. Scale is the proportion of the model trains compared to the real thing. An accurate O scale model is 1/48th the size of the real thing. If the track gauge is 4 feet by 8½ inches, the exact 1/48 scale of that would be 56.5 inches divided by 48, which is 1.18 inches. Modelers round that off to 1.25 inches or 1¼ inches—the distance between the railheads on all of Lionel's O (and O-27) track.

That scale also applies, of course, to the locomotives, cars, buildings, and people. Lionel has always played fast and loose with the scale of its toy trains. Lionel was producing O Gauge trains for more than 30 years before it introduced the Scale Hudson in 1937. That was Lionel's first 1/48 scale model, and it was soon followed by a 0-6-0 in 1939 and a boxcar, tank car, hopper, and caboose in 1940. Lionel did not produce another true O scale model until about 1985.

In the meantime, Lionel did produce toy trains to run on O Gauge track, but with bodies, chassis, and wheels much smaller than 1/48 scale. The smaller-size models were better able to negotiate the tight curves of Lionel's track, and they were considerably less expensive to produce. Perhaps the grossest examples of Lionel ignoring scale proportions are the huge signals that are closer to 1/24 scale than 1/48 scale, and the

Ken Huber's Standard Gauge layout with a No. 120 Tunnel, a No. 124 Station, a No. 436 Power Station, and a Lincoln Log cabin.

Left to right: Lionel's Standard Gauge, Large Scale, O Gauge, and HO Scale models.

The blue steam locomotive is larger than the Standard Gauge green observation car because it is built to about 1/22 scale, while Standard Gauge is about 1/31 scale. The green Standard Gauge stock car is obviously built to a larger scale than the observation car. Remember, these were toys.

The Lionel No. 8E Standard Gauge electric locomotive was based on a full-size locomotive that operated through the Hoosac tunnel on the Boston & Maine Railroad. The 11-inch model, produced between 1925 and 1932, was one of the smaller Lionel Standard Gauge engines.

men who came out of the Automatic Gateman sheds (see page 84) would be nearly 18-feet-tall giants if they really were O scale.

Lionel has confused the O scale concept considerably over the years by offering a variety of sizes labeled O-27, O Gauge, O Scale, Standard O, and O-72. All of these will run on Lionel's three-rail track, but the longer locomotives and cars will not be able to negotiate curves any smaller than 54- or 72-inch diameter without derailing.

Lionel also has offered toy and model trains in HO (1/87 scale), OO (1/76 scale), S (1/64 scale), O (1/48th scale), Standard Gauge (about 1/31 scale), and G (1/22.5 scale—Lionel calls it Large Scale) configurations. Lionel even offered

a train in the tiny N scale (1/160) as part of the Lionel Big, Rugged Trains in 2000, but they were nonpowered and designed to run on the bare floor.

Recently, most of Lionel's models are accurate height and width according to scale, but they are often shorter than accurate scale. The shorter models look a bit more realistic when the trains travel around the too-tight curves. And, the shorter models are less likely derail on those tight curves than longer, correct-scale-length models.

However, it is the Standard Gauge trains that Lionel produced in 1930s that are historically the true classics of toy trains, which is why Lionel called them Lionel Classics when it began to produce the current series of replicas in 1988.

Opposite page:
Lionel's massive Standard Gauge Lionel No. 408E electric locomotive in front of a No. 124 Station on Ken Huber's layout.

THE CLOCKWORK TRAIN

Lionel's 1934 Mickey Mouse Circus Train featured an animated Mickey. The locomotive was powered by a clockwork mechanism much like a windup alarm clock.

Today, we assume everyone always had electricity in their homes, but that was not true in the early 1930s. As a result, electrically powered toys were extremely rare and very expensive at the time. In fact, the power for most mobile toys came from a mechanism derived from the mechanical clock.

Today, few clockwork mechanisms, outside of cheap kitchen timers, exist, but for the first half of the twentieth century, these mechanisms were used in a variety of devices, including toy trains, cars, and boats.

Here's how they worked: You inserted a large key and cranked until there was more resistance than you could overcome. When the mechanism was wound up tight, the stop lever was released and the toy would travel forward at top speed.

These types of clockwork mechanisms first appeared on German-built trains in the 1800s. In fact, Lionel's founder, Joshua Lionel Cowan, had some of these clockwork-powered trains as a child.

Lionel used a clockwork mechanism in the 1934 windup Lionel circus train featuring Mickey and Minnie Mouse. The set included a locomotive, a tender, and three cars for just $2. Lionel also offered a windup handcar with Mickey and Minnie that sold for just one dollar. In contrast, the top-of-the-line Lionel *M10000* streamlined train was priced at $25 in 1934. Lionel sold enough of those dollar circus trains to rebuild its business during the Great Depression. And of course with each of the circus trains came a brochure describing the magic and wonder of the more expensive Lionel electric trains.

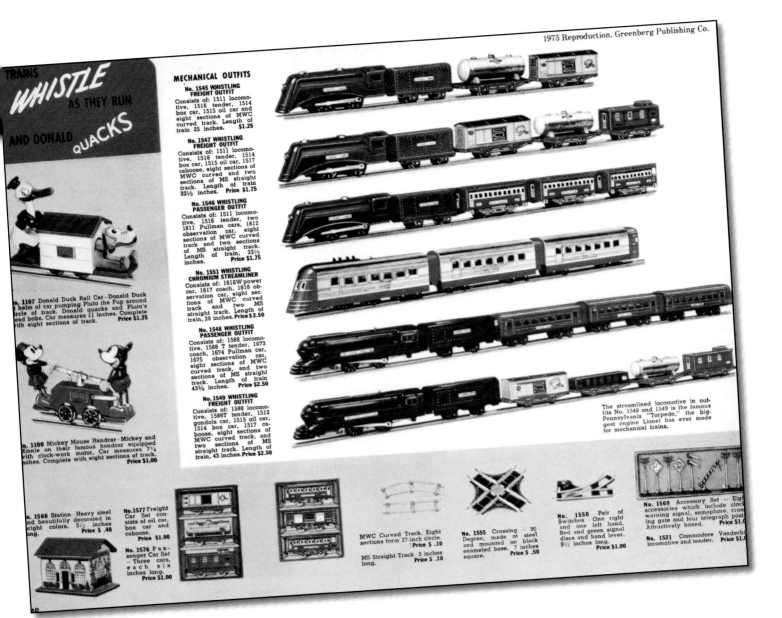

Lionel also offered handcars with Mickey and Minnie pumping. All of these train sets are powered with clockwork mechanisms, and most of the cars have just four wheels.

LIONEL'S EARLY ENTRY-LEVEL SETS

Lionel has long offered lesser-expensive train sets designed and priced for the budding toy railfan. In some of its earliest entry-level train sets, the boxcars, stock cars, gondolas, and cabooses had four wheels (a design feature that faded from American railways in the late 1800s) because with fewer wheels, they were cheaper to produce. In 1926, the four-wheel series was upgraded by adding a hopper car, flat car, and, in 1930, a manual dump car (that was later enlarged and adapted to remote control).

The four-wheel series was upgraded again in 1939 to include a bright orange Shell tank car. These cars were as attractive as their larger eight-wheeled counterparts, with bright colors and plated parts.

In 1940, the compact four-wheel cars allowed Lionel to offer a train set for about $5 compared to $25 for the *M10000* streamliner and $97.50 for the massive scale New York Central 4-6-4 Hudson with four scale freight cars.

Prior to World War II, the most expensive Lionel sets and individual cars and locomotives were the Standard Gauge items, which were much larger than even the Scale Hudson and

freight cars. Later, Lionel differentiated between the mid-range O Gauge products and the cheaper stuff by producing somewhat lighter track for the O-27 train sets, which also came with smaller and less-expensive cars.

Some of these cars were simplified versions of the larger cars. They had fewer pieces, and most of the details were simply lithographed (printed) on the stamped-steel sides. These lithographed cars were offered with four wheels and with eight wheels and were, apparently, designed to provide an even lower-cost alternative to the more complex four-wheeled cars.

Lionel did not bother to include many of the lower-cost train sets and cars in its catalogs. Since the 1920s, the lowest-priced train sets have been sold by department stores and chain stores.

Today, you can see bargain-priced entry-level Lionel train sets in most of the big-box stores, in dozens of mail-order Christmas catalogs, and, of course, in hobby stores. Most of those sets are priced as low as possible and are part of Lionel's O-27 or Traditional O series. Today, an entry-level Lionel O-27 set might sell for under $200, with the better sets at about $500. The largest sets for collectors approach $3,000.

Lionel's brightly painted and plated four-wheel tank car from 1939 was one of its last four-wheeled cars.

Compare the size of Lionel's No. 807 Four-Wheeled Caboose (upper right) to the No. 2657 Eight-Wheeled Caboose (upper left). The No. 2682 (lower) is a lithographed car.

Lionel's series of 1939 entry-level cars included four-wheeled versions of the company's larger cars, like this No. 807 Four-Wheeled Caboose and No. 809 Manual Dump Car.

EARLY TINPLATE LOCOMOTIVES

The locomotive has always been the icon of railroading, and Lionel took particular care to create engines that looked like the massive machines they were to emulate. But somehow, Lionel's locomotives made these replicas designed for work look like machines designed for pure fun.

Lionel's locomotives also were designed shorter, proportionally, than their width and height, so they could get around the miniature track's tight curves easier (if the curves were the same scale as the locomotives, the curves would have to be large enough to go around the outside of entire house). Lionel kept these same almost-comic proportions whether the locomotive was Standard Gauge or the smaller O Gauge.

Whenever possible, Lionel selected locomotives that were already bulldog compact, one of the reasons why replicas of electric locomotives were so common in the Lionel line. It was possible to re-create a full-size electric locomotive with the length actually being close to the same proportions as

the width and height. The steam locomotives that Lionel's models replicated usually had six large driving wheels, while Lionel's only had four. Similarly, Lionel's steam locomotives often were short two or four leading wheels and two or all four of the trailing wheels.

Lionel's largest locomotives of the 1920s and 1930s were more or less replicas of the real railroad's 4-6-4 Hudson locomotives, like the famous *Blue Comet* train's power. Lionel's *Blue Comet* was missing two drivers, but it was huge even though it was only a 4-4-4. That design allowed Lionel to shorten the model by about a fourth.

For the lesser locomotives, Lionel dropped pairs of leading and trailing wheels, so the most common Lionel engines were 2-4-2s. The "bread and butter" steam locomotives of the Lionel line, the engines that pulled the lower-priced sets that outsold impressive Standard Gauge sets, were usually simple 0-4-0s (no leading or trailing wheels and four drivers) with eight-wheeled tenders.

Ken Huber's 2-4-2 Lionel No. 1835E Steam Engine was made from 1934 through 1939. The No. 385W Tender is gunmetal in color and did not come with the engine originally, but was with the set when purchased from the original owner in the late 1990s.

The Lionel No. 1668E from 1937 was one of the first locomotives to use a die-cast superstructure rather than previously stamped-steel products. The locomotive has the modern "torpedo" styling to emulate the Pennsylvania T-1 (a massive 4-4-4-4 that Lionel made in exact scale 70 years later), but this version was a short but trim 2-6-2.

Lionel's Standard Gauge steam locomotives had removable stamped metal flags on the pilots. On the real railroads, the flags were usually used to indicate that the train was being followed by another, or that the train had priority over most others on the line.

THE *BLUE COMET*

The Lionel *Blue Comet* passenger train was patterned after the Central Railroad of New Jersey's train in more than its design. It even featured the same names of the coaches as the real *Blue Comet*. On the other hand, the real-world *Blue Comet* was just an upmarket commuter train, but Lionel put its version right beside the cross-country fliers like the *20th Century Limited* or the *M10000*.

Lionel offered several versions of the *Blue Comet*, ranging from a train that was part of a medium-priced O Gauge set to the Standard Gauge *Blue Comet*, part of the largest set Lionel offered. In 1931, Lionel produced one of the largest locomotives in its history to pull the three-car *Blue Comet*. The Standard Gauge 400E light blue 4-4-4 with a round Vanderbilt tender was nearly 30 inches long. Lionel reproduced the massive locomotive, tender, and three cars in 1990, as one of the first in the company's Lionel Classics series.

Fittingly, the most sought-after locomotives that Lionel gifted with the *Blue Comet* name matched the configuration of the full-size locomotive. Steam locomotives are categorized by the number of wheels and drivers, starting with the num-ber of small pilot wheels at the front, followed by the number of the large drivers or driving wheels, then by the number of small trailing wheels that support the firebox. If, for example, a locomotive has four pilot wheels, six drivers, and two trailing wheels, it is designated as a 4-6-2, which the railroads refer to as a Pacific. The locomotives that pulled the full-size *Blue Comet* were CNJ Railroad class G-3a 4-6-2 Pacifics, numbered 831, 832, and 833.

Lionel's trade ship Standard Gauge *Blue Comet* model was missing two of the massive drivers (and had an extra trailing wheel), thus was a 4-4-4. The stamped-steel O Gauge version of the *Blue Comet* was missing even more wheels. It had just two pilot wheels, but it did have two trailing wheels (a 2-4-2). Lionel also reproduced this stamped-steel O scale *Blue Comet* with that 2-4-2 locomotive, a Vanderbilt tender, and three cars in 1991. Lionel also offered the locomotive with a square tender, both painted black. Lionel did not offer an accurate-scale replica of the *Blue Comet* until 2002, and then, although the locomotive finally was a 4-6-2, it was not an accurate replica for the Jersey Central locomotive.

A Lionel No. 1835E Standard Gauge steam locomotive with a 385W tender pulling a No. 310 Baggage Car, a No. 309 Pullman Car, and a No. 312 Observation Car served as a stand-in for the *Blue Comet* on Ken Huber's layout.

ALL NEW
COLLECTOR LINE
STANDARD GAUGE BLUE COMET
The flashy Blue Comet express passenger train began operation on the Jersey Central line in 1929, providing a crack New York to Atlantic City run. In advertisements it was claimed that the brilliant paint, "blends the restful blue of the sky and ocean with the cream-tinted warmness of the sand beach." Offered originally on the Lionel line in the 1930's, this train's coaches were named after comets, indicative of the speed by which the Blue Comet traveled.
6-13103 BLUE COMET STEAM LOCOMOTIVE AND TENDER
One of the most handsome locomotives ever offered by Lionel, the original #400E ran with a four-wheel pilot truck, four drivers and a four-wheel trailing truck. Our resurrection of the classic Blue Comet is painted in two-tone blue with nickel plated brass accents.
THE 1-400E LOCOMOTIVE FEATURES: • Durable enamel finish • Nickel plated brass accents • Formed steel and die-cast metal construction • "E" unit for forward-neutral-reverse operation • Original style "Bild-A-Loco®" motor • Operating red firebox glow • Operating headlight • Latch style coupler on the tender
Pack: 3 Wt.: 55 Cube: 7.2
6-13408 BLUE COMET PASSENGER CARS
#1420 "FAYE" PULLMAN
#1421 "WESTPHAL" PULLMAN
#1422 "TEMPEL" OBSERVATION
ALL PULLMAN CARS FEATURE: • Durable enamel finish • Nickel plated accents • Formed steel and die-cast metal construction • Opening doors • Detailed interior • Metal passenger seats that swivel • Two washrooms and restrooms with opening doors • Removable roofs for interior access • Illuminated interiors
Pack: 3 (1 each of 3) Wt.: 20 Cube: 5.2
#1420 "FAYE" PULLMAN
#1421 "WESTPHAL" PULLMAN
#1422 "TEMPEL" OBSERVATION
34
35

Lionel produced a far more accurate Standard O replica of the New Jersey Central *Blue Comet* in 2002.

The O Gauge *Blue Comet* that Lionel offered in 2001 has the correct-style 4-6-2 locomotive and reasonably long cars, but somehow lacks the romantic appeal of the stamped-steel toy version.

LIONEL

THE TINPLATE PASSENGER CARS

Three of Lionel's massive Standard Gauge stamped-steel cars on Ken Huber's layout.

Lionel produced stamped-steel passenger cars from the early 1900s through most of the 1940s. The first of those stamped-steel cars were mostly massive Standard Gauge cars, perhaps not quite as gigantic and handsome as the *Blue Comet* cars, but large 18-inch-long cars.

The problems of way-too-tight curves forced Lionel to shorten all of its passenger cars to much the same effect as Lionel's steam locomotives. The passenger cars on the full-size railroads were an average of about 86 feet long, which if reduced to 1/48 scale (Lionel's nominal proportion for its O Gauge models) would result in a model that was over 21 inches long. Some real-world coaches were just 60 feet long, which would have produced an O scale model 15 inches long. Lionel's were just over 9 inches.

The absurdly tight curves also forced Lionel to mount the couplers on the trucks, rather than on the body. That forced Lionel to raise the car above the trucks, so the couplers would be able swing beyond the width of the body. It is those shortened lengths and elevated car bodies that make toy trains look like toys.

Interestingly, Lionel's Standard Gauge passenger cars were, proportionally, longer than O Gauge counterparts by about 10 percent. The top-of-the-line Standard Gauge car was about 18 inches long, twice as long as the similar O Gauge model. Lionel apparently wanted to make it visually clear that Standard Gauge was not only larger, but more closely matched the proportions of the prototype.

Lionel's lithographed passenger cars had little three-dimensional detail, especially around the doors and window frames. Those details were reproduced with paint like on these No. 1690 and No. 1691 cars from 1937.

The red car is a No. 630 O Gauge Observation Car made between 1924 and 1932 that would have been included in one of the lowest-priced electric train sets. The larger car is a Standard Gauge No. 490 Observation Car made between 1923 and 1932.

Lionel reintroduced a number of its stamped-steel cars after World War II, including these 6440 Series cars that were first produced in 1938. These were similar to the 600 Series cars of 1933, but had two more windows.

TINPLATE FREIGHT CARS

It is easy enough to forget how long Lionel has been around until you look at some of its earliest products. Lionel's tinplate-era cars have re-created individual wooden boards and rivets on the steel cars, both features found on real railroad cars of the 1920s and 1930s. The design looks more realistic in that it's made of metal, rather than plastic pretending to be metal.

The cars in Lionel's catalogs were almost always stamped from heavy-gauge steel, plated, then painted. Lionel did, however, produce thousands of cars that were intended for the mass market. These were cheaper versions for cheaper train sets, so their bodies were often just a single deeply drawn piece of metal. Usually, the boxcars had separate doors and door slides, but the other details such as ladders and brake wheels were simply printed on with the lithograph process. Most manufacturers, including Lionel, eventually dropped these less-expensive cars, but other toy firms, like Marx, continued to make lithographed cars into the 1950s.

The Lionel No. 116 Ballast Car, made between 1910 and 1926, is about the size of a small loaf of bread.

Lionel's earliest Standard Gauge cars were often replicas of the then-current wood cars on the real railroads, like this No. 114 Boxcar with No. 112 Gondola Car from 1912.

The four-wheeled No. 805 Boxcar in the upper left would have been included in the least-expensive electric-powered sets from 1927 to 1934. The No. 1679 car on the left was only a bit more costly because it had lithographed details rather than separate parts. The bottom car is a Standard Gauge No. 514, the biggest and best boxcar you could get.

This No. 513 Standard Gauge Cattle Car was made from 1927 to 1938. The No. 514 Refrigerator Car was made from 1929 to 1940. Both cars have opening doors.

SEARCHLIGHT CARS

Lionel's series of searchlight cars might seem like stretching the company fantasy too far. The real railroads did, in fact, use floodlights to illuminate work areas for track repairs and, of course, to right wrecked trains. However, these floodlights did not light up the sky; rather they just spread a broad beam focused ahead.

Lionel offered cars with two searchlights in both Standard Gauge and O Gauge from 1931 until 1940. After World War II, Lionel introduced a variety of different designs with single searchlights, including a standard flatcar and a depressed-center flatcar, each carrying an imitation electrical generator. Lionel also offered some searchlights on flatcars and inside boxcars with two-foot-long cables so that the light could be positioned alongside the tracks.

The searchlight cars are fascinating to watch, especially when running the train in the dark. The locomotive headlight lights up the way ahead, and the interior lights in the passenger cars (or caboose) flash across the carpet.

The Lionel Standard Gauge No. 520 Floodlight Car was made between 1931 and 1940.

Lionel used a depressed-center flatcar for one series of searchlight cars. This one is from 1952. The generator was just a plastic molding. The cars picked up their power from the third-rail roller in the center of the trucks.

Lionel's current Maintenance of Way Remote Control Searchlight Car and Pennsylvania Searchlight Car are simply new and relettered versions of cars first seen in the 1950s.

The unusual No. 3530 Electro-Motive Power Car has a simulated generator inside with a portable spotlight that is connected to a lighting pole, as seen on Michael Ulewicz's layout.

WRECKING CRANES

One of the joys of playing with toy trains is that they sometimes, completely by accident of course, wreck. Not one to miss a chance at launching another successful product, Lionel began producing a "work" crane, which fans all knew was really a wrecking crane, in Standard Gauge in 1926.

In 1931, Lionel introduced in the No. 2810 Working Crane in O Gauge. It was a re-creation of a much larger prototype. In 1938, Lionel added a smaller O Gauge crane, No. 2660, which was similar in its proportions to the earlier Standard Gauge crane. The smaller crane was re-released in 1946. The small cab and boom were also used on Lionel's earlier magnetic cranes.

In 1946, Lionel introduced the first of its die-cast cranes. The model was fitted with massive six-wheel trucks as an Operating Derrick Car and was a shortened re-creation of a much heavier prototype crane. Later, lower-priced versions were fitted with four-wheel trucks. Again, the cab was used on the Lionel magnetic cranes.

All of Lionel's cranes had a cab that could swivel 360 degrees, a boom that could be raised or lowered by turning a wheel on the back of the cab, and a hook that could be raised or lowered by turning a second wheel on the side of the cab. It wasn't exactly push-button control, but many a kid spent endless hours trying to upright a wrecked car or locomotive using just the hook on the crane and those two hand wheels.

Lionel made railfans' dreams come true in 2003 with the exact-scale TrainMaster Control Crane Car that allowed completely hands-off operation of the crane anywhere on the track using the TrainMaster Control system, detailed on pages 216 and 217. In addition to cab swiveling, boom raising, and a big hook moving up and down, the model allows a second hook to be operated by remote control, and the crane even has it own floodlights aimed at the boom. The model will also uncouple anywhere with TrainMaster Electrocouplers.

The real cranes need telescopic outriggers on each side for stability, and, yes, the Lionel TrainMaster Control crane car has those, as well. Lionel also produces a 50-foot flatcar with shed and toolboxes as a work caboose for the scale crane car.

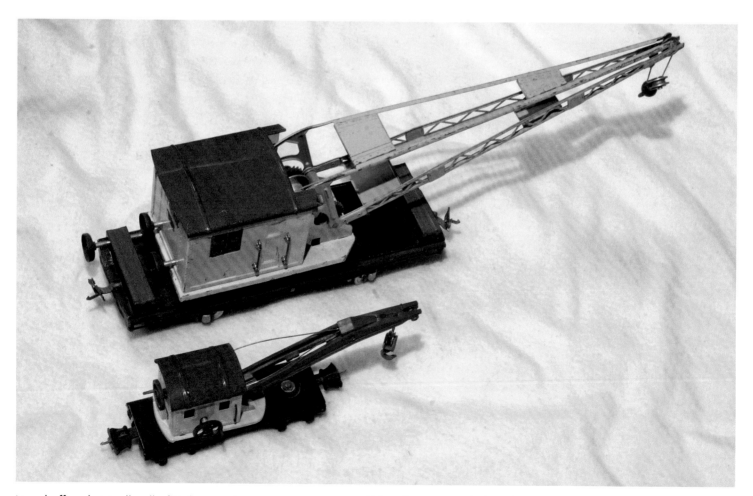

Lionel offered virtually all of its locomotives, passenger cars, and freight cars—including the crane—in both Standard Gauge and O Gauge, such as these unrestored examples from Chris Gans' collection at Nicholas Smith Trains in Bloomall, Pennsylvania.

Lionel introduced the first of the six-axle Operating Derrick Cars in 1946 and has reproduced them many times in a variety of railroad names, including several variations in the Lionel Lines series, like this one on Vito Glimco's layout.

The exact-scale TrainMaster Control Crane Car in operation on Oliver Gaddini's layout.

TINPLATE CABOOSES

For the children who grew up in the first three-quarters of the twentieth century, the caboose was a rolling substitute for an imaginary tree house or clubhouse. Millions of boys and girls waited beside the tracks, often on a planned trackside excursion, to see a train pass with its red caboose bringing up the rear.

If the locomotive looked like out-of-control power, then the caboose somehow brought that power under control. It was quieter than the front or middle of the train, and cabooses had a homey feel.

Lionel knew all about this fascination with the caboose, of course, and offered an astonishing array of cabooses over the years. The stamped-steel tinplate cabooses of the first half century were the most colorful of these and somehow were even more representative of places where kids (rather than adults) might hang out.

Lionel's first series of Standard Gauge cabooses mimicked, rather than replicated, the Pennsylvania Railroad's class N5 two-window cabooses (the Pennsy called them cabins) with centered cupolas. Lionel offered a rather crude version in 1906 and upgraded it in 1926. The company produced essentially the same car in O Gauge in 1926 and made one with four wheels in 1927.

Lionel finally introduced a nearly accurate Pennsylvania Railroad caboose in 1940. The 1940 version was still stamped steel, but had accurate proportions (at about 20 percent scale). Lionel's first accurate scale model of the N5 was its OO, or 1/76 scale version, in 1938.

However, the centered cupola caboose was only one of a dozen different cabooses Lionel has offered. The company has also produced a variety of offset-cupola cabooses in both tinplate and die-cast with scale proportions. Lionel has also offered bay window cabooses and work cabooses (the body of a short four-wheel caboose on a flatcar) to provide a resting place for overhanging boom on the wrecking cranes.

Lionel produced this offset-cupola No. 517 Standard Gauge Caboose from 1927 to 1940 in two shades of green and red.

Lionel's No. 117 Standard Gauge Caboose from 1912 was closer to the then-current prototypes than you might imagine.

One of the alternate all-red paint schemes for the 1927 Lionel No. 517 Standard Gauge Caboose (left) compared to its O Gauge No. 2657 car from 1946.

LIONEL POWER STATIONS

Lionel's trains have always been large, heavy, and powerful. Some were certainly heftier than others, but those massive trains required a lot of electricity to get a train that might weigh 30 pounds moving down the rails. For most of the first half of the twentieth century, a Lionel electric train was considered a marvel in the science of electricity. In those days, only the electric trolleys in streets and some of the full-size electric locomotives had more electrical power; in a word, Lionel was awesome.

When Lionel issued its first catalog in 1902, the electric trains inside were powered by homemade "wet" batteries or massive dry cell batteries. Lionel did not offer a transformer to convert 110-volt house current to a less suicidal 20 or 30 volts to operate the trains until 1914. Lionel's early transformers and train control switches were state of the art at the time, with simple knife-style switches or pivoting contacts. Even the speed control was a series of a half-dozen tabs that could be contacted by the throttle lever—far short of the 200 steps of almost seamless increases in speed possible with today's Legacy Command Control.

Because electricity was still something most kids held in awe in the early 1900s, Lionel created stamped-steel

Top: The Lionel Type K transformer (center) could be housed inside the No. 436 Power Station (left). A No. 91 Circuit Breaker (not connected) is shown at the left.

Bottom: The skylight could be removed from the Lionel No. 436 Power Station to allow access to the speed control lever on the transformer.

With the roof in place, the No. 436 Power Station becomes just part of the scenery. The No. 80N semaphore was made from 1936 to 1942.

power stations to hide the transformers and switches. These industrial buildings were replicas of the real-world electricity-generating plants, with smokestacks for the imagined steam engine inside.

One of the most collectible of all the Lionel tinplate products was the spectacular No. 840 Industrial Power Station, which was produced from 1928 to 1940 (one is visible on the far left of the bottom photo on page 73). This 26-inch-wide and 18-inch-tall structure was designed to hide two transformers and had six knife-style switches inside to control the power to lights and other accessories.

Lionel also offered several more affordable power stations, like No. 436, that were small enough to house a single transformer.

The control panel for Ken Huber's Standard Gauge layout uses two Type R 110-volt Lionel transformers from the 1940s, four 1925 vintage controllers for the No. 222 Remote-Control Turnouts, and a direction/whistle controller.

THE METROPOLITAN STATION

The most famous of the Lionel railroad stations was the company's majestic stamped-steel Illuminated Metropolitan Station, first produced in 1936. The station was one of Lionel's first "action" accessories. It included an automatic train-stopper circuit, so trains would automatically stop for a moment or so and then proceed with no help from the operator. Lionel dropped the station from its line in 1950, but it reappeared in 2003.

Lionel produced two versions of these magnificent stations: the No. 112, with a single window on each side of the main doors, and the No. 116, with four windows on each side. The smaller two-window version was also offered from 1928 through 1940 as the magnificent No. 128 Illuminated Metropolitan Station Terminal and Terrace with an 18x31-inch elevated (with six scale steps) simulated marble terrace (painted stamped steel), eight outside lights, interior illumination, a cloth flag, and the automatic train stop feature.

Lionel reissued both the No. 128 and the same building with train-stop feature in 2003 as part of the Lionel Classics series.

The larger station is the No. 116 with four windows on each side. The smaller is the No. 112.

The No. 124 Station (missing the two exterior light fixtures) and No. 58 Lamp Post on Ken Huber's Standard Gauge layout.

The Lionel Classics reproduction of the O Gauge tinplate No. 128 Illuminated Station and Terrace on Richard Kughn's Lionel layout.

STATION PLATFORMS

Over the years, Lionel has offered a wide choice of stations, but in most towns and cities there's more to the railroad scene than just the station. Most stations also have long platforms along the tracks to protect the passengers from the weather as they wait or walk from the station to their waiting coach or Pullman car. At some commuter stops, there is no station, just the covered platform.

On the real railroads, the platforms are often 1,000 feet long, but few Lionel layouts have more than a foot or two of space for each "town." So Lionel's passenger platforms always have been only about 12 to 18 inches long. Lionel's first station platform was the 18-inch-long No. 155 that Lionel labeled as a freight shed.

Lionel has offered these covered platforms both with and without lights. In 1956, Lionel reintroduced one of the longest-running products in its line, the 12-inch-long No. 156 Illuminated Station Platform with a green base, a red roof, and a simulated wrought-iron fence down the center with room for four small billboards. Lionel has reproduced it several times with and without the fence and with and without lights.

In the modern era, real railroad passengers often wait inside glass-enclosed sheds, and Lionel has, of course, produced one of its own, the No. 34102 Amtrak Station.

Two Lionel No. 155 Freight Shed platforms on Chris Gans' Standard Gauge layout.

The original No.156 Illuminated Station Platforms from 1956 had red roofs and green bases through most of the 1940s and 1950s.

Some modern versions of No. 156 Illuminated Station Platform have gray roofs and brown bases.

THE HELL GATE BRIDGE

Feats of fantastic engineering were headline events in the 1920s and 1930s, with structures like the new Empire State Building topics of daily conversation. One such news-making structure was Upper Manhattan's Hell Gate Bridge, which opened in 1917 to allow northeastern New England rail traffic to reach New York City more efficiently. The steel arch that got its name from the turbulent waters of the East River and Hudson River below spanned 977 feet—about 20 feet when reduced to O scale.

Lionel made its version of the Hell Gate Bridge in 1928; it was stamped steel and a massive 30 inches long. It was considered an engineering marvel in the toy world at the time. In the past 10 years, Lionel has reintroduced the Hell Gate Bridge in several variations of the Lionel Classic series.

In 2006, the Milwaukee Lionel Railroad Club also re-created the Hell Gate Bridge in near-accurate 1/48 scale on the upper deck of its massive Lionel layout so that all could see how the real bridge dwarves the massive railroad locomotives that cross it.

The Lionel Classics reproduction of its 1928 Hell Gate Bridge on Bill Langsdorf's FasTrack layout.

This is an O scale re-creation of the Hell Gate Bridge on the Milwaukee Model Railroad Club layout.

The Lionel Classic replica of the Hell Gate double-track bridge on Richard Kughn's layout.

TINPLATE BRIDGES AND TUNNELS

No matter what, toy trains eventually travel in circles. That's a fact that Lionel fans have long tried to avoid by using all manner of devices, from long straights to figure eight–style overpasses, in their layouts. Yet what seemed to work best to break up the possible monotony of going around and around and around was to throw in a few bridges and tunnels, so the trains actually traveled through and over something.

Bridges and tunnels were part of Lionel's earliest offerings. And because there really was nothing to bridge, Lionel designed most of its bridges to simply slip between the bottom of the ties and the carpet, floor, or flat tabletop. Adventurous modelers, following lovely illustrations in *Model Builder* magazine, cut ragged foot-wide slots in their tabletops to give the bridges something to span.

Beginning in 1931, Lionel offered two basic styles of open-top truss bridges: the No. 270 style with rectangular sides and the ends angled at 45 degrees and the No. 280 series with taller sides that formed three sides of an octagon. The No. 314 solid-plate girder-style bridges did not appear until 1940.

Tunnels were a bit more of a challenge to add to a layout, since they needed mountains to bore through and few layouts had the space for a scale-size mountain. Lionel solved that issue by making the outside of the tunnel just a few inches larger than inside. Lionel offered at least four different versions of these U-shaped, upside-down troughs that were all about 7 inches wide and 7 inches high. They varied in length from 8 to 20 inches.

Lionel designed these tunnels large enough to clear Standard Gauge trains, as well as slightly smaller O Gauge versions. There was plenty of space on the outside of the tunnels for simulated scenery. The No. 120 had room for two snow-capped peaks, as well as a winding road up one side that crossed two road bridges and had a small hotel (all to about 1/300 scale, of course). Lionel also offered some larger square-shaped tunnels with the two tunnel portals 90 degrees apart and the surrounding mountain high enough to cover the curved track and a train. These ranged from about 18x16 inches to 23x40 inches, and all were discontinued just before World War II.

Lionel produced these steel truss bridges for both Standard Gauge and O Gauge layouts. This is the No. 280 Bridge and a No. 120 Tunnel on Ken Huber's Standard Gauge layout.

Peter Perry has combined modern FasTrack and current Lionel trains with 1930s-era accessories, including one of the shorter No. 119L Tunnels, upper left, the small No. 1023 Straight Tunnel, and one of the larger No. 120L Illuminated Tunnels. The small bungalow in the center was part of a set of five Lionel offered in the 1930s. The Landscaped Diner is at the lower left.

The Standard Gauge No. 120L Tunnel from 1927 has two snow-capped mountain peaks, with a road and a hotel on one side.

STOP THAT TRAIN!

A Standard Gauge No. 408E Electric Engine approaching a No. 80N Semaphore on Ken Huber's layout.

For motorists and pedestrians, a track's crossing signal always caught your attention, especially if a train was approaching or passing. For the railroad engineers, however, it was the semaphore or searchlight signal that was the most important because those signals were what prevented one train from crashing into another. And, of course, Lionel's generations of young engineers knew that because one of the secret pleasures of playing with toy trains is the possibility that a wreck might occur.

Lionel, of course, had signals available within its first years of production. At first, the signals were activated manually. In 1923, Lionel patented the use of one of the outside rails to act as a contact to actuate a highway crossing sign. That same year, the company introduced the No. 76 Block Signal. Three years later, in 1926, Lionel introduced the No. 80 Electronically Controlled Semaphore for Standard Gauge and the smaller No. 080 version for O Gauge, both operated by the train passing over a track section with an insulated rail.

By 1927, Lionel had introduced both the No. 99 Block Signal and Semaphore Signal that could be set to illuminate the red light (and lower the arm on the semaphore) to stop the approaching train. After a few moments' wait, the train could proceed. This would happen each time a train came

to the signal, unless you manually turned off the signal (to a constant green).

In 1940, Lionel introduced a true automatic train control signal, the No. 153, which was a small electronic train control system unto itself. It could be wired to prevent two trains running in the same direction from colliding nose to tail. Two trains could be operated in the same direction on the same track (assuming, of course, you had a transformer large enough to handle them and they ran more or less at the same speed—independent control of two trains had to wait until 1995 when TrainMaster Command Control arrived). If the second train began to catch up to the first, the signal would change to red and stop the second train.

To get the automatic block signal to work, the track needed to have Lionel's insulated track pins and at least three signals, even on a simple oval. Yes, this really was railroad engineering (but not the work of the pull-the-throttle-type of engineer. See the wiring diagram on page 192 of *The Lionel Train Book* and *The Big Book of Lionel*).

Lionel produced dozens of different signals and signal bridges—some just dummies, others with lights but no control, and others with lights that were activated by trains but provided no train control.

A Lionel No. 384E Standard Gauge Steam Engine about to activate a No. 068 Warning Signal.

LIONEL'S TRACK

For more than a hundred years, Lionel has battled to convince its customers that three rails are better than two. From the standpoint of a real railroad, the concept of having a third rail down the middle of the track is absurd. However, die-hard Lionel fans argue that many real railroads that use electric current rather than diesel fuel or coal for energy have a third rail, but that third rail is on the outside of the track, suspended about a foot in the air on pedestals.

Lionel battled over the concept of two rails versus three with American Flyer in the toy train business for 50 years, but Lionel now owns American Flyer and it is Lionel's three rails that have survived. The simple explanation for the success of three rails is that the design is structurally more substantial than just two. Toy train track is constantly being disassembled and reassembled, stepped on, and kicked, so being sturdier matters.

Lionel's track uses sheet-steel rails that are formed to create a tube with two flanges. Steel pins are inserted in the tubes to join track sections together. The flanges of the tubular rails are clamped to metal ties with stamped-metal clips. Those three steel-pinned joints in solid stamped-steel rails are stronger than two rails.

The three-rail system also simplified wiring on complex layouts. The two outer rails are positive charged, and the lone inner rail is negative (or vise versa). With two rails, one rail must be positive and the other negative. That can cause problems when track is configured into a reverse loop because the outer rails will create a short circuit. Lionel's three rails sidestep that problem completely.

Lionel did produce two-rail track for the smaller OO Gauge in 1940, and recently Lionel has offered straight and curved two-rail track for American Flyer. With those two exceptions, millions and millions of sections of Lionel three-rail track have been manufactured, and it all performs very nicely indeed.

A Standard Gauge No. 222L Remote Control Switch (the railroads call them turnouts) attached to a 20x45-degree crossing on Ken Huber's layout.

Lionel's O-31 remote-controlled switches and track with extra wood ties and blackened rails on the Chicagoland Lionel Railroad Club's layout. The track with brown ties is Lionel's lighter O-27 track with same track gauge as its O Gauge track.

Two-rail track for American Flyer models, Lionel's O-31 track, and the Lionel FasTrack. The FasTrack has the realism of two-rail track with the operating simplicity of three rails.

The large curve on Lionel's remote control O-72 switch allows longer locomotives and cars to operate without derailing.

STANDARD GAUGE LAYOUTS

The train layout dreams of boys and girls in the 1920s and 1930s are coming true for many Lionel collectors today. Here are two examples of how grownups now play with their Lionel Standard Gauge trains:

Ken Huber not only managed to retain the Standard Gauge train set passed down to him by his father, but also expanded it. In a bit of a time warp, his home has a finished attic with room for the 7x15-foot railroad, much like the illustrations in Lionel's *Model Builder* magazine in the 1930s.

Chris Gans has a consuming passion for Lionel in general, but Lionel Standard Gauge in particular. His layout includes virtually every accessory Lionel produced prior to World War II, with two concentric ovals of Standard Gauge track and about eight switches. If you wonder what Lionel's catalogs would look like if you really could see everything they made in one place, take a look at Chris Gans' 10x30-foot layout. The only significant missing items from Lionel's prewar era here are two No. 923 Lionel Curved Tunnels that Chris is restoring.

Both of these layouts are built the way Lionel suggested in *Model Builder* magazine and in Lionel's long-out-of-print *Handbook for Model Builders,* with framework much like a patio deck, screwed-together from 1x4s and covered with half-inch plywood. Short-bristle carpet covers the plywood on Chris Gans' layout to provide a more natural setting and to somewhat deaden the sound.

Ken Huber's 7x15-foot Standard Gauge layout has enough track for two trains to operate at once while a third is waiting on a siding. The locomotives and cars are from the 1930s with a few period toys like the Lincoln Log house.

Chris Gans' 10x30-foot layout incorporates virtually all of the accessories Lionel produced for the pre–World War II period. The No. 128 Illuminated Metropolitan Station Terminal and Terrace in the foreground with a string of Lionel No. 280 Red Bridges and No. 120 Tunnels on the far right.

The No. 124 Station is in the foreground on Chris Gans' layout with two of Lionel's No. 438 Signal Towers to its left and, in the lower left, the Hell Gate Bridge, which was large enough to accommodate Lionel's Standard Gauge trains. Lionel's huge No. 840 Industrial Power Station is visible at the extreme left.

BOATS, AIRPLANES, AND AUTOMOBILES

Lionel has reproduced its pylon airplane in many forms, including as Santa Claus in his sleigh with his reindeer.

Lionel has always been in the toy business, so that does not mean the company has only produced toy trains. Lionel also manufactured toy boats, airplanes, and automobiles.

Lionel's two stamped-metal speedboats, both with clock-work mechanisms, debuted in 1933. Several variations of them were offered through 1941. The boats also were reproduced in 1991 as part of the Lionel Classics range of repro stamped-steel toys. The two boats had nearly identical hulls, but the original No. 45 had the pilot and passenger in the front and No. 4 had the pilot and passenger in the rear with intake stacks of twin V-8 engines directly in front of them.

Lionel also was one of pioneers in slot car racing, introducing a stamped-steel set in 1912. Lionel reproduced the set in 1991. Each car ran on is own 30-inch or 36-inch radius curve with a trough in the center, and a standard Lionel steel rail ran in the bottom of the trough. The sides of the trough provided positive current, the rail negative current. Lionel was also one of several importers of the British-made Scalextric

1/32 scale slot cars in the early 1960s. Then Lionel tooled and produced its own 1/32 scale sets with cars and track similar to Strombecker's in 1962. Later the company produced HO-size electric cars in the early 1960s and somewhat larger PowerPassers that were steered like toboggans by the walls of a trough track in the set.

Lionel's first airplane was a pylon flyer with a tower or pylon providing the power via a motor inside driving a vertical shaft. A thin wire was attached to the top of the shaft parallel to the ground, and the airplane was mounted on the end of the wire. When the motor spun the shaft, the airplane flew around the pylon on its wire tether. The wire to the airplane could also be tilted up or down so that the plane could climb and dive and take off and land. With some practice, the plane could even be controlled cleverly enough to perform loops.

Again, Lionel promoted the plane heavily, with the models demonstrated in theater lobbies for the new 13-episode *The Mysterious Pilot* serial. In 1936, every boy who could manage to find a nickel for a ticket was at the theater waiting for "the next thrilling episode" of these serials. Unfortunately, they could only buy the pylon flyer from 1936 to 1939.

Lionel has released a series of a much simpler pylon aircraft over the last decade, ranging from a simple private airplane to Santa Claus with his reindeer and sled, a witch on a broom, Dumbo, the World War I airplanes of Snoopy and the Red Baron, a pair of World War II fighters, and, most recently, an army helicopter. These newer pylon fliers simply go around and around—the swoop and dive features of the earlier version were not reproduced.

Snoopy and the Red Baron chase one another on this version of Lionel's pylon airplane accessory.

Lionel's first pylon airplane from 1936 was able to move up and down for landings and to perform aerobatic maneuvers.

Lionel introduced clockwork-powered speedboats in 1933, and they were reproduced in 1991.

PART III
THE PREWAR BOOM

THE STREAMLINED FUTURE

Lionel's 1934 *M10000* passes Lionel's 2006 exact-scale recreation of the Milwaukee Road's *Hiawatha* on the Milwaukee Model Railroad Club layout.

For some Americans in the 1930s, the future was all they could look forward to. With the Great Depression clearing out the savings of many and putting even more out of work, the future certainly couldn't be worse than the present. Hoping for better days was often the way to see the calm in the storm.

To help create optimism about the country's future, the nation's railroads introduced several new passenger trains that were styled like something from a Buck Rogers story.

With their clean lines and futuristic elements, the passenger trains of the late 1930s were as newsworthy as putting a man on the moon was a few decades later. The Union Pacific Railroad got lots of press attention with its futuristic *M10000*, which debuted in 1934. On a demonstration tour across the country, the *M10000* attracted an estimated 15 million people in 22 states. Wisely, Lionel had its own sleek *M10000* model out soon enough that it could be displayed alongside the full-size train as it toured the country on demonstration runs.

Within months of the Union Pacific's *M10000* introduction, the Burlington Railroad put its *Zephyr* into operation, and again Lionel had its replica available within months (actually the Lionel's train was a re-creation of Boston & Maine's *Flying Yankee* but essentially the same train).

Despite these smart marketing decisions, Lionel still struggled in the Depression, going into receivership in 1934. However, as the country's economy recovered, so did Lionel. And a major part of that recovery was boys willing to convince their dads to pay for their own replicas of those *M10000* and *Flying Yankee* streamlined passenger trains.

The *M10000* was a significant part of Lionel's history because it used a number of die-cast parts (pieces created in a female mold from a molten mixture of zinc and tin). Using this method was far faster than fabricating the same intricate parts from several stamped-steel pieces. The resulting parts were usually much more realistic, but the dies for the cast parts were far more expensive to cut. It also was the company's first accurate scale model, but it was 1/45 scale, about 5 percent larger than true 1/48 scale.

One of the most famous toy trains was Lionel's replica of one of the first streamlined trains, the Union Pacific *M10000* articulated passenger train of 1934. Lionel introduced the model the same year the real train began operation.

The first streamlined passenger trains featured very distinctive observation cars like those on the Union Pacific 1934 *M10000* and the Milwaukee Road's *Hiawatha*.

THE STREAMLINED *HIAWATHA*

Time and time again, Lionel used innovative marketing techniques to push sales of its products, and with the 1934 introduction of company's series of streamliners, Lionel showed just how well it targeted customers.

For its Midwest and western customers, the company offered the Union Pacific *M10000* streamliner. For the eastern market, Lionel produced the Boston & Maine *Minuteman*, rather than reproducing the near-identical Burlington *Zephyr* (see page 82), which would be poplar in the Midwestern market. In 1937, Lionel targeted the Midwestern market by offering a replica of the Milwaukee Railroad's *Hiawatha*.

Lionel's *Hiawatha* utilized the same cars as the *M10000*, so it was not a true replica of the full-size *Hiawatha* streamliner, but close enough. The full-size *Hiawatha* cars were not articulated. Each had its own pair of four-wheel trucks and couplers. Also, the *Hiawatha* train's observation car was not the rounded shape of Lionel's *M10000* substitute.

Lionel reintroduced the *Hiawatha* in 2006, but this one is near-correct 1/48 scale, with cars nearly twice as long as the original Lionel model (and twice as accurate—right down to the unique Milwaukee Road fluting on the sides). Lionel's newest *Hiawatha* also re-creates the slanted end of the observation car that has become know as the "beaver tail" car.

Lionel also offered the *Hiawatha* as a Standard Gauge train for the first time in 2001, as part of the company's Lionel Classic series. This was one of the most accurate of all the Lionel Standard Gauge toys, with the cars and locomotive having proportions almost as exact as the O version, but with proportionally shorter cars coupled a bit further apart.

Lionel's exact-scale *Hiawatha* from 2006 on the Milwaukee Model Railroad Club layout.

The 2006 version of the *Hiawatha* has full interiors and lighting.

Lionel's latest products, produced in China, include full interiors with a half-dozen passengers in each car.

The restrooms inside the *Hiawatha* include replica toilets.

THE *ZEPHYR*

The streamlined train that most clearly fulfilled Americans' ideas of the future in travel was the Burlington Railroad's *Zephyr*, introduced in 1934. While the *Zephyr* was somewhat smaller in profile and the cars were a bit shorter than those on standard passenger cars, it had a shocking finish. The entire train was covered in brightly polished stainless steel, with ribs or corrugations on the sides to provide even more of a fantasy-like spectacle.

Its streamlined design and futuristic look made it front page news in nearly every newspaper in America. Of course, it didn't hurt that on the *Zephyr*'s run from Denver to Chicago, it averaged 77.6 miles per hour, hitting 115 miles per hour on the way.

The three-car *Zephyr* train was put into full-scale operation in 1935, a year after Union Pacific's *M10000*. Lionel had its O Gauge model of Boston & Maine's *Flying Yankee* in service that same year. Because the Budd Company had

The Lionel 2004 reproduction of its 1935 *Flying Yankee* in operation on the Chicagoland Lionel Railroad Club's FasTrack layout.

$12.50

WITH BUILT-IN WHISTLE and CONTROLLER $16.50

LENGTH OF TRAIN 42 INCHES

THE *Flying Yankee*

● **No. 267E "O" GAUGE REMOTE CONTROL STREAMLINE OUTFIT**
This Lionel Flying Yankee is an accurate reproduction of the silvery streamliner of the Boston and Maine. Cars are heavily chromium plated and fluted. Outfit consists of: No. 616E Distant Control power car, two No. 617 Coaches, No. 618 Observation car, No. 88 Reversing controller, eight sections of OC curved track, four sections of OS straight track and Lockon. Train is 42 inches long. Track forms oval 50 by 30 inches. **Price $12.50**
Type "B" Transformer will operate this train. Type "T" will provide for many accessories.

No. 267 W. Same as No. 267E but with real railroad whistle equipment and with No. 66 whistle and reversing controller instead of No. 88. **Price $16.50**

No. 616W. Motor car unit only, with built-in whistle and No. 66 whistle controller. **Price $10.00**
No. 617. Coach with one vestibule. Fluted, chromium plated finish. **Price $3.75**

The Yankee power car has a chisel-edged prow.

Cars are coupled into vestibules that contain tiny lights.

In the end of the train is a round solarium lounge with curved, wide-vision windows.

Lionel used a minimum amount of artistic license to present the *Flying Yankee* in the 1940 catalog.

manufactured the car bodies of both the full-size *Zephyr* and the *Flying Yankee*, the trains were nearly identical. The full-size *Flying Yankee* differed from the *Zephyr* primarily because the first car in the *Zephyr* was a baggage mail car and the first car in the *Flying Yankee* was another coach. That first *Zephyr* also had just three cars, but eventually a fourth was added.

The Lionel model was shortened to operate on tight 32-inch curves. It also had its *Flying Yankee* lettering on the nose and with Lionel Lines displayed on the sides. Lionel reproduced the stamped-steel version of the train in 2008 as a Lionel Classic.

In 2004, Lionel produced an exact-scale replica of the original cast-metal three-car *Zephyr* that was 49 inches long (the four-car tinplate version was just 42 inches long).

The real-world *Zephyr* also became a movie star, playing the lead role in the 1935 film *Silver Streak*. The movie was remade in 1976 (using Canadian equipment) starring Gene Wilder and Richard Pryor to introduce the fun of riding trains to a new generation.

One of the original *Zephyr* trains is on display at the Chicago Museum of Science and Industry, while one of original Boston & Maine *Flying Yankee* trains is being restored in Lincoln, New Hampshire.

Lionel also offered a lower-cost O-27 version of the *Zephyr* in 1935 as the *Fluted Chrome Streamliner* with each car having its own two pairs of trucks.

THE AUTOMATIC GATEMAN

The products that Lionel introduced in 1935 helped set the company on the track it would follow into the next millennium. The operating whistle—albeit in a separate station, not the locomotive—appeared in that year, as did the most fascinating and enduring action accessory, the Automatic Gateman. Even into the 1970s, the gateman who slid out with his lighted red lantern each time a train passed remained a Lionel icon.

Lionel offered the Automatic Gateman in variety of colors and with some rather odd workmen, like on the Thomas the Tank and Friends version where Sir Topham Hatt slides out of the shed as the trains roll by.

Each Lionel Automatic Gateman was a product of the era in which it was produced. The first units, from 1935 to 1938, included a diamond-shaped "Look Out for Locomotives" railroad crossing signs that matched the signs of that period on the real railroads. Later versions had the familiar cross bucks. The gateman was molded in a phenolic resin until 1950, when injection–molded plastic was used. The earlier sheds and warning signs were also metal,

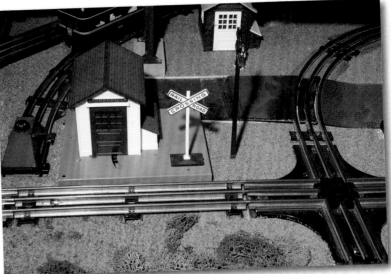

Most of the Automatic Gatemen's sheds had red roofs, but in 1951 the roof was brown.

The 1947 Automatic Gateman still had the stamped-metal shed, and the gateman's arm could swing with the illuminated lantern.

but plastic was substituted to create a somewhat more realistic building and workman (although he was still about 15 feet tall).

Most of the automatic gatemen carried an illuminated lantern, but some of the lower-priced versions had just an unlit plastic lantern. The accessory was activated by Lionel's metal connector that was placed beneath track. The weight of the train would push on the metal contactor so that two separate metal strips (contact points) would touch to open the electrical circuit. There was an adjusting knob, but the device relied on weight.

Unfortunately, nearly every Lionel locomotive had a different weight, so getting it loose enough for heavier locomotives but not too loose for the lightweights was an endless task. If you understood Lionel's system, you could also actuate the device by providing an insulated outside rail as the contact to provide much more reliable operation of the accessory.

With the base removed, you can pull up on the steel gear rack to allow it engage the proper teeth on the round pinion (spur) gear to synchronize the door's closing with the gateman being at rest.

The Standard Gauge No. 1405 Gateman moved his arm up and down as the train passed.

THE O SCALE HUDSON LOCOMOTIVE

Prior to 1937, Lionel had never made an accurate-scale model of any locomotive, passenger car, freight car, or accessory, except the *M10000* streamliner. There was no need to because both the boys and fathers playing with Lionel sets had become accustomed to toy trains being caricatures of the real thing. The toys' inaccurate shapes were usually the result of producing the locomotives, cars, and accessories from stamped-steel sheet. There was only so much you could do with steel stamping, especially when re-creating the fine details you could find on real trains.

However, a number of small manufacturers were making a limited number of kits to re-create dead-accurate exact 1/48 scale replicas of steam locomotives, electric locomotives, and freight and passenger cars in the 1930s. These were nearly always sold as kits that contained a pile of rather crude castings and bits of wood and metal. If you wanted an accurate model, you had to build it yourself from that box of bits.

Lionel also had no specific scale for its models. The company had dozens of locomotives, cars, and track that were called O scale, but the length, width, and height of these conformed to no specific proportion of the prototype. O scale was supposed to be 1/48 the size of the real thing, but Lionel's models varied from about 1/50 scale for the width and height to 1/60 scale for the length. Lionel's models also had wheel flanges that were about 10 times larger than 1/48 scale.

Lionel's first truly accurate locomotive was the Scale Hudson, so named for its accurate proportions to the original. The wheel flanges on the Scale Hudson were much smaller, although about four times correct scale. Still on present-day O scale and HO locomotives, the oversize flanges remain.

During the 1930s, serious model railroaders removed the third rail from the center of the track and placed a much smaller third rail beside the track. This outside third rail was actually true to prototype, as it was used by many of the commuter lines in Northeast Corridor. The enthusiasts who built their track with outside third rail used near-scale rails and ties. Lionel's Scale Hudson was designed for easy adaptation to an outside third rail. Lionel offered the Hudson with the then-current Electromagnetic box couplers and large flanges for three-rail. The company also offered the Hudson with close-to-scale-size wheel flanges, scale couplers, and wiring for two rails, as well as provisions for the pickup shoes for the outside third rail. The Hudson was also available as a kit for the true hobbyist.

The Hudson was so popular that Lionel introduced many replicas with smaller tenders, superstructures, and chassis. Some were almost as accurate reproductions as the Scale Hudson, but the dimensions were all reduced to create a smaller-scale model of about 1/55 scale. No exact scale

could be determined because Lionel designers had to match the necessary wheel or drivers' sizes, complete with the massively oversize wheel flanges, to create the running gear, then create a superstructure with proportions that were as close to exact scale as possible.

The next-smaller scale for model railroads is S scale, which is 1/64 the size of the real thing. Many of Lionel's reproductions are much closer to 1/64 scale than to accurate 1/48 scale. And Lionel offers the entire range of toys, from an very increasing line of exact 1/48 scale locomotives and cars to replicas of the 1950s-era O-27 Lionel toy trains, that really are close to 1/64 scale and re-creations of the American Flyer toy trains (these, except for the oversize wheels flanges, couplers, and the necessary space to clear them, were usually exact 1/64 scale).

The 763E was included with some of Lionel's top-of-the-line sets.

REMOTE-CONTROL UNCOUPLING

Lionel had been demonstrating the magic of remote-controlled electric trains for 30 years in department store window displays when customers demanded even more remote-control action in the mid-1930s.

Yes, no longer would the electric warning signals introduced in 1921, the automatic crossing gate and illuminated block signals that came out in 1923, and the semaphore signal that appeared in 1926 do.

In 1938, Lionel introduced remote-control couplers that would couple anywhere and uncouple over a special electronic track section. The first remote-controlled couplers were a development of the box coupler from 1936 that, in turn, was a development of the automatic latch coupler of the 1920s. The 1920s-era coupler was a development of the simple hook-and-eye coupler from the days of clockwork trains.

The hook-and-eye couplers worked fine if the train was being pulled, but when backing up, the hook would sometimes disengage. To solve that problem, Lionel added a latch in 1938. The latch could be pushed open automatically by simply pushing one car against the other—assuming, of course, that couplers were perfectly lined up, which they only were about one time in a hundred. Still, uncoupling was a complicated task of trying to hold the hook with one finger while flipping up the latch and simultaneously pulling the cars apart. Lionel solved that patience-sapping uncoupling sequence with the box coupler in 1936, where the latch was replaced with a simple open-ended box that would gather the opposite hook to make it far easier to couple the cars. To uncouple, you just lifted up the box.

The next step was remote-control uncoupling in 1938. The new 1938 coupler had a small magnet on the bottom of the box. The uncoupling track was an electromagnet between the rails (a device that continues to this day). When the push button on the control panel was pressed, the electromagnet energized and would pull down the box of any coupler parked over the electromagnet to open the coupler.

After World War II, Lionel developed an automatic coupler that was a near-exact replica of the knuckle-style couplers used on real railroad cars.

Lionel offered three different methods of operating the couplers. First, on the higher-priced O scale or Standard O models, the coupler was activated with its own wire-wound magnet. The cars (or a car coupled to a locomotive) needed be positioned anywhere along the special 10-inch-long remote-control track that had five rails. A single small pickup shoe was suspended from the bottom of each truck, positioned over one of those fourth or fifth rails (later versions had a metal

Lionel trains from the 1920s used this combination coupler to couple with either latch-type or hook-and-eye couplers.

plate that contacted both fourth and fifth rails). The shoe picked up the electrical current to open the coupler. When you pushed the uncoupling button, the current activated the coupler's electromagnet that opened the coupler. These electronic couplers would only operate with the special control box that was included with the remote-control track.

The second alternative coupler was Lionel's truly advanced (for the time—it being 1946) electronic-control coupler. With this system, a radio frequency signal was transmitted to a small receiver inside each car. The cars could be uncoupled anywhere. The same system allowed automatic dump cars that were equipped with an electronic system to be dumped anywhere on the track. Lionel again offered "uncouple anywhere" capabilities when TrainMaster was introduced in 1995. With this system, a radio signal triggered the system, allowing cars to be uncoupled (or dumped) anywhere on the layout.

In 1948, Lionel introduced the third type automatic coupler, a less-expensive version of the knuckle coupler.

However, this version had a small steel disc about the size of a penny below the coupler. This coupler was triggered by a No. 6019 Magnetic Track (later called an operating track) that was a 10-inch straight track with an electromagnet grafted into the center rail. The electromagnet was activated by a remote-control push button.

Lionel also offered a manual actuated uncoupling ramp with the less-expensive sets that could be clipped beside the track, so the metal disc could be pulled down manually. Lionel called it the Manumatic control.

Lionel now has a fourth version of its automatic coupler. Most of the newer Standard O locomotives have ElectroCouplers that can be uncoupled with the usual remote-control track or anywhere on the track with TrainMaster or Legacy.

All of the Lionel couplers have retained the massive size that was introduced in 1945. Lionel does, however, include scale-size couplers with exact-scale freight cars so that the cars and locomotives are appealing to the hi-rail modelers who operate scale-size models on three-rail track.

A hook-and-eye coupler on the left and combination coupler on the right, uncoupled.

A hook-and-eye coupler on the left and combination coupler on the right, coupled.

In the 1930s, the latch-type coupler was modified for automatic coupling to create this "box" coupler.

Lionel's exact-scale freight cars are furnished with Lionel's latest automatic knuckle couplers (left), as well as a body-mount Lionel magnetic automatic scale coupler (right). Yes, Lionel's couplers are and always have been grossly oversized!

LIONEL'S SMALL SCALE

Today, HO scale models constitute about 80 percent of the model railroad market. Lionel recognized the potential of small-scale trains early on, and in 1938 offered a stunning collection of OO scale models just a bit larger than HO scale. Lionel's 1938 OO scale line included an OO scale replica of the New York Central Hudson that Lionel had offered in exact O scale the year before, plus a boxcar, gondola, tank car, and caboose.

OO is 1/76 scale and, at the time, it was a wise choice for Lionel because it was the most popular of the smaller scales. Lionel's OO scale was described as 5/32 of an inch to 1 foot, which is only partially accurate. True OO scale is 4 millimeters to 1 foot, and 4 millimeters is about .15745 inches and 5/32 of an inch is about .1562 inches, a difference of .001 inch. These proportions made Lionel's OO Hudson 15¼ inches long while Lionel's O-27 Hudson was 17½ inches long and considerably bulkier than the OO scale Hudson. The majority of Lionel's trains operated on 31-inch-diameter curves, but the two-rail OO curve was 48 inches in diameter.

The OO scale boxcar was similar to the Pennsylvania Railroad's class X-29 40-foot single-door car, and it was offered in Pennsy lettering. The offset-side 34-foot two-bay hopper had opening hopper gates and came in gray or black with Southern Pacific or Lionel Lines markings or in black with Reading markings. The single-dome tank car was available in black with Shell markings or in silver with Sun Oil (Sunoco) markings. The caboose was based on a Pennsylvania class N-5 prototype and was available in New York Central or Pennsylvania markings.

Lionel offered the OO series as both a relatively less-expensive three-rail with less detail (and a 27-inch-diameter curve) and a two-rail exact scale (with that 48-inch curve). The two-rail track had scale-size ties, close to scale-size rail, and included ballast. Today, only the HO track from Marklin in Germany can match it for detail. The three-rail track had slightly larger rails, but it was still the most realistic track Lionel had made until FasTrack was produced more than 60 years later. The three rail had only one curve and straight, but did offer a pair of switches.

Lionel clearly considered OO to be for hobbyists rather than children because the products were extremely well detailed and exact scale. In fact, the locomotive and each of four cars could be purchased as either ready to run or as kits.

The Lionel OO scale Hudson was available set up for two or three rail, and it was offered as a kit or ready to run.

The Lionel OO scale tank car was offered in either Shell or Sun Oil (Sunoco) markings.

Lionel offered this same Pennsylvania Railroad Class N-5–style OO scale caboose as an O Gauge model in 1946.

Lionel featured its then-new OO Gauge Hudson and a boxcar on a two-rail layout on the cover of the October 1939 issue of *Model Builder*.

MODEL BUILDER

OCTOBER, 1939

10¢

Lionel used the same layout photographed on the cover of the October 1939 issue of *Model Builder* to cite the advantages of OO scale in this advertisement.

LIONEL "OO" GAUGE

...runs rings 'round the small gauge train field!

BRINGS GREATER ACCURACY, DETAIL AND POWER TO TABLETOP RAILROADING

A gem in its beauty and a brute in its strength, the Lionel scale model Hudson is geared and gaited to modern power ideas and precision-built to exacting scale model standards. Model builders everywhere are talking about the sensational performance of this monarch of the midgets, now available for operation on either two-rail or three-rail track and with or without the Lionel built-in locomotive whistle.

Send at once for a copy of the new 1939 Lionel catalog and find out why "OO" gauge is so rapidly mounting in popularity. See new Lionel "OO" gauge car kits with accurate car markings; new electric switches; new "OO" train outfits in a wide range of prices; new, realistic track with accurate ties and two solid steel rails. Don't delay. Send for catalog at once. Address The Lionel Corporation, Department BT, 15 East 26th Street, New York, N. Y.

NEL TRAINS

131 E. GRAND AV.
NEW HAVEN, CONN.
14—19

Workin' on a Railroad...just to pass the time away

BUILD 'EM TINY ... BUILD 'EM MIGHTY ...
TWO LIONEL SCALE MODELS!

WHERE SPACE IS UNLIMITED
Giant "O" Gauge scale model Hudson, so superb in its accuracy and detail the president of the New York Central Railroad uses it as an ornament in his office.

WHERE SPACE IS LIMITED
The biggest little train ever made, 14½ inches of "OO" Gauge scale model perfection, duplicating every detail of its big "O" Gauge brother and ingeniously constructed so it will circle a track only 27 in. in diameter.

CONSTRUCTION KITS FOR "O" GAUGERS
A NEW SCALE MODEL ENGINE FOR "OO"

Whether your railroad system is "O" Gauge or "OO" you can now own a Lionel scale model Hudson, for now this masterpiece of all miniatures comes in both scales.

Lionel's giant, 24½-inch "O" Gauge reproduction has already endeared itself to the hearts of every true scale model railroader. Now, for the first time, model builders may buy this engine of the Century as easily as on a time-payment plan. For it can be bought in five separate kits, one at a time or all at once. Five kits, $59.50. Five dollars extra for the sixth kit which contains the remote control whistle and whistle controller.

What detail, accuracy and expert construction Lionel has put into the "O" Gauge Hudson will be found

also in the "OO" miniature.
For it has been made from exactly the same designs and blueprints. 14½ inches long and driven by worm-gear motor, it's a veritable power plant on wheels, as smooth in its performance as any engine ever made. "OO" Gauge scale model freight cars. True-to-scale, bakelite-mounted, easily assembled "OO" track. Switches. Crossovers. In fact, everything you need to be a "OO" Gauge railroader.

Start now. Write at once for a copy of the new 52-page, full-color Lionel catalog that pictures the complete "OO" Gauge line, tells you all about the Lionel scale model "O" Gauge kits. Act at once. Clip and mail coupon today.

CUT OUT ▼ AND ▼ MAIL ▼ TODAY

The Lionel Corporation   Dept. Z
15 East 26th Street, New York, N. Y.

Enclosed is 10 cents for a copy of the new 1938 52-page, full-color Lionel Catalog. Send it to:

Name_____

Address_____

City_____ State_____

Couple up with LIONEL
FOR ALL THE THRILLS OF RAILROADING

Lionel made a side-by-side comparison of its new O scale Hudson and the OO scale version in the February 1939 issue of *Model Builder.*

ACTION FREIGHT CARS

After Lionel introduced remote-controlled track switches ("turnouts" is the railroader's term), kids couldn't just get enough of steering a train onto a siding or another set of tracks. So Lionel not only introduced remote-controlled uncoupling in 1937 (so kids could dump cars at will), but also came out with the first of many remote-control coal-loading towers (see page 100) that year.

With these, you could dump a load of coal into a bin, and a conveyor would carry it to an elevated hopper where it could be dumped into another coal car. The device was very similar the coaling towers then in use to refuel the tenders of steam locomotives. However, no Lionel steam locomotive had real coal or the space for it (that area was usually occupied by the motor-driven steam whistle, or today by the electronics for TrainMaster or Legacy and RailSounds).

For 1939, Lionel introduced a series of four automatic-unloading cars: a coal car, a log car, a barrel car, and a boxcar—all worked by remote control at the push of a button. With these, Lionel could brag that you could control the train itself, run the train from the mainline to a siding through a track switch, operate a whistle, couple or uncouple, and load or unload freight cars all by remote control. What excitement!

Lionel did not dribble out this series of "action" freight cars, but offered four of them at once. The most famous was the No. 3859 O Gauge electrically operated Remote-Control Dump Car, a development of the hand-operated dump car Lionel had offered for decades, but with a solenoid mounted in a box on the end of the car. The new dump car was intended to feed (and to be fed by) the new No. 97 Electric Remote-Control Coal Elevator, which had been in production

The Lionel No. 3652 Barrel-Dumping Gondola had swing-up sides that were actuated by remote control.

since 1937. In 1946, Lionel offered the No. 3459, another all-metal coal dump car with mechanism beneath the car like that used for the remote-control log car. Lionel reintroduced this one in 2002, along with a re-creation of the similar No. 3461 Log Dump Car.

The other cars offered in 1939 were the No. 3811 Remote-Control Log Car, the No. 3652 Barrel-Dumping Gondola, and the No. 3814 Merchandise Boxcar that ejected boxes. Dozens of additional action cars were produced over the next 70 years, but those first four were the breakthrough products. All four cars were activated by some remote-control track section that was also used to trigger the new automatic couplers.

With the introduction of these, a boy or girl railroader could stop the train, turn the track switch from mainline to siding, back up to position the coal car at a coal elevator, uncouple from the car to head back onto the mainline to couple onto the remainder of the train, and head on down the line. Meanwhile, the load of coal could be dumped into a coal elevator's waiting bin, and the coal elevator could be commanded to start moving that load of coal up into its storage bin. And all of this action takes place by moving a remote throttle, hitting a remote reversing switch, pushing a remote uncoupling button, and pushing the coal elevator's operating button.

The No. 3459, another all-metal coal dump car with the operating mechanism housed beneath the car.

The most common Lionel coal dump cars are the "button-operated" cars like this Union Pacific No. 6-36811 Coal Dump Car. The steel button or disc hanging beneath the car was pulled down by an electromagnet to trip the lever on the car so that the car could dump its load.

The Lionel Operating Hopper Car was reintroduced back in the 1990s to be used with the No. 456R Operating Coal Ramp.

Lionel introduced this new O scale Operating Coal Dump Car with the mechanism beneath the car in 2000.

Lionel often advertised its catalogs in *Model Builder* magazine, like this ad for the 1938 catalog for just a dime. The big news, then and now, was remote control.

LIONEL'S ACTION INDUSTRIES

Four action accessories on Richard Kughn's layout, including three coal-loading accessories: the red-and-green structure in the foreground is the No. 497 Coaling Station, the beige structure with a red roof is the No. 97 Coaling Station with chain-belt buckets to hoist the coal into the tower, and the angled gray conveyor of the No. 397 Coal Loader just visible behind it. The green, yellow, and red accessory is the Log Loader.

L ionel went beyond the ends of the railroad track ties to re-create the world the railroads served early on, offering passenger stations and platforms from the very beginning. However, it wasn't until the late 1930s that Lionel began to re-create the industries—like coal, lumber, steel, and cattle—the road served.

The first industry to be included in Lionel's model railroad world was the coal industry. Among the items Lionel produced to add "coal" to your layout were accessories where you could accept dumped coal from automatic cars, with the coal then carried by conveyor to a waiting bin to be dumped into another empty car.

In 1938, Lionel introduced its first remote-controlled electric coal accessory, the No. 97 Elevated Coal Storage Bunker. Coal could be dumped into a bin on one track and reloaded into a waiting hopper car or gondola on an adjacent track. A chain was fitted with small buckets to dig the coal from the bin, move it over the elevated coal bunker, and then dump it into the bunker. A second button opened the gate in the floor of the bunker to allow the coal to spill out into a waiting gondola or hopper car. The sound was also very realistic with loud clashing and clanging, as the buckets moved around the chain's drive sprockets and the bucket dug into the waiting pile of coal. Lionel has reproduced No. 97 Coal Storage Bunker many times over the ensuing seven decades and the new ones are just as noisy as the originals, the coal just as messy, and the thrill just as great in knowing you are re-creating a railroad at work by merely pushing a button.

Real coal is pretty dirty stuff, and Lionel certainly did not expect its customers to blacken their hands like a real engineer or fireman. So Lionel produced artificial coal that was forever a clean, shiny black.

The No. 97 Electric Coal Elevator has been reproduced several times to maintain a steady supply of Lionel's oldest operating accessory.

Lionel has reproduced the No. 456 Operating Coal Ramp that automatically uncouples the car from the train and opens the hopper doors.

The Lionel No. 456 Coal Ramp can be used with the No. 397 Coal Loader to provide push-button unloading and reloading.

Lionel has produced several other coal loaders. The disadvantage of No. 97 was that it required two parallel tracks, which was not always that simple to arrange on some Lionel layouts. The No. 397 Diesel Operating Coal Loader, introduced in 1948, had a rubber conveyor belt with bars that lifted coal, so it could be dumped into the same car (or, more realistically, in the same car after the car made a trip around the layout and back).

In 1950, Lionel introduced the No. 456 Coal Ramp, which was a reasonable replica of the type of coal ramps used at some real railroad locomotive coaling towers, as well as at hundreds of retail coal dealers in a time when most of America's homes were heated by coal furnaces. The accessory was dependant on a hopper car with operating bottom gates like a full-size hopper car. Lionel produced the car especially for this accessory.

The No. 456 also had a bin that collected the coal. You could simply carry the bin to an empty hopper car and dump

the coal back in. It was far more interesting, however, to use the No. 397 Diesel Operating Coal Loader, positioning it so its receiving bin was below the hopper on the No. 456 Trestle. The coal could then be loaded by the No. 397's conveyor belt so that the whole operation was hands free (as was the No. 97; but this was at least as realistic a variation on the coal unloading-loading process—in part because real railroads did not use side dump cars for coal. They used hoppers with bottom gates and the ever-more-sophisticated model railroaders knew it).

The most bizarre of Lionel's coal loaders has to be the No. 497 Coaling Station. This accessory was introduced in 1953. With this accessory, the coal is dumped into a bin, and the entire bin is hoisted by a pair of cables to the top of the structure. At the push of a button, the bin is tilted and the coal dumped into a second stationary bin. The gate in the floor of the bin then can be opened by remote-control push button to dump the coal into another empty hopper or gondola.

The red-sided structure is Lionel's No. 497 Coaling Station, with a No. 97 Electric Coal Elevator into the background, and an American Flyer Seaboard Loader to the right on Oliver Gaddini's layout.

THE MAGNETIC CRANES

Lionel produced the No. 165 Magnetic Crane with a small cab in 1940 and brought it back after World War II. Henry Speth's model is at work on Bill Hitchcock's layout.

Lionel replaced the small cab on the magnetic crane with this larger cab in 1946.

The metal platform on the magnetic crane was replaced with a plastic frame that simulated the rolling "gantry" cranes in 1954.

One of the most interesting and realistic Lionel accessories is the company's magnetic crane. The model operates almost exactly like the prototype, except of course you are making it perform by remote control.

Lionel introduced the first of the magnetic cranes in 1940. The design allowed the crane to be rotated 360 degrees and the magnet, suspended on cables, to be raised or lowered and energized to pick up any ferrous materials. The boom could be raised or lowered by a crank on the back of the cab.

The No. 165 versions of this crane produced during the 1940 to 1946 period had stamped-steel cabs. Later No. 182 versions had much larger cast-metal cabs. In 1954, the No. 282 Gantry Crane was released. It performed the same functions but was mounted on a plastic gantry with rollers on each corner. The full-size gantry cranes rolled on individual rails, but Lionel did not provide the rails. Raising or lowering the boom was the only effective way of moving the electromagnet closer or further from the track.

In 2002, Lionel offered the No. 24134 Crane with a clamshell bucket that was closed by the magnet. The clamshell could scoop up coal much like that type of prototype.

If one crane is good, two are better. At the push of a button, the magnet picks up ferrous metal and when the button is released, the load is dropped.

LIONEL'S BASCULE BRIDGE

Bridges are the most exciting scenery on a Lionel layout. They become even more so when they are designed to swing upward, lift, or pivot to allow tall boats to pass through them. Over the years, Lionel re-created every style of moving bridge, from swing-up bascule bridges and elevator-action lift bridges to the rotating swing bridges.

Lionel introduced the first No. 313 Bascule Bridge in 1940, and gloriously it was back in 1946 through 1949. The 21-inch-long bridge was made of stamped steel and was designed to sit on a tabletop. It included an automatic circuit stop for the train when the bridge was lifted. It was reintroduced in 1997.

Lionel produced a much lower-grade version of the Bascule Bridge in 1975, the beginning of the General Mills Fundimensions era. This No. 2317 Drawbridge had the mechanism beneath the track, so the track was elevated about three inches above the tabletop. This is the bridge that is on the cover of the *Lionel Train Book* from 1986. A

similar but simpler version that only elevated the track two inches was introduced in 2002.

The Lionel Operating Lift Bridge was announced in Lionel's catalog back in 1950, but never produced. Lionel has offered two versions of it, though: The larger version was produced in 1992 and was 29 inches long and 19 inches high with rectangular vertical end towers. In 2002, a slightly smaller version debuted. It was 26 inches long and 15 inches tall with tapered end towers. Each works similarly. The bridge is lifted upward, guided by the two end towers, with cables and a winch with counterweights. Then the trains are stopped automatically, and the horn sounds as the bridge is being raised.

To round out the moving bridge spectrum, Lionel produced a rotating or pivoting 40-inch-long (including the two 4-inch-long approaches) swing bridge in 2003 with a massive replica of a steel truss bridge that pivoted horizontally 90 degrees to let ships pass through.

The two versions of the Lionel No. 313 Bascule Bridges on Richard Kughn's layout are placed side by side to span a small harbor inlet.

The double-track No. 6-12782 Operating Lift Bridge on Richard Kughn's layout is one of the largest models Lionel has produced. This was the first of Lionel's lift bridges—the second has tapered vertical end supports like the bridge in Lionel's 1950 catalog.

LIONEL'S LUMBER INDUSTRY

Most Lionel railroaders group as many action accessories as they can on parallel tracks. Robert Babas has the unloading platform for a Lionel Operating Milk Car opposite the log bin on the Lionel Log Loader. The cattle pen for the Operating Cattle Car is visible to the left.

Lionel knew that playing with trains would be heaps more fun if commodities could actually be loaded and unloaded. Hence, the operating coal and log loaders and dozens of other operating "industry" accessories.

Lionel was able to re-create the majority of the wood industry, from cut logs to cutting lumber and shipping and receiving boxes (the company even produced a motorized pair of lumberjacks cutting up a tree). Eventually, Lionel had accessories to re-create the path of a log from its source to a crate.

The No. 164 Lumber Loader was Lionel's first lumber industry operating accessory, and it required two tracks, like the No. 97 Coal Elevator. Again, model railroaders asked for a log loader that could be used on just a single track.

So, Lionel designed the No. 364 Conveyor Lumber Loader, produced from 1948 to 1957, to sit alongside a single track. The logs could be unloaded at the bottom conveyor, and a belt carried them up to a waiting rack at the top. At the push of a button, the vertical posts at the edge of the ramp would drop and the logs would roll off onto a waiting car. The accessory was made of stamped metal, and the vibration of the motor and belt created a racket almost as loud as the chain-driven No. 164 Loader.

The Lionel No. 464 Lumber Mill, introduced in 1956, re-creates the effect of logs being sawed into lumber. Later, Lionel also offered a re-creation of the American Flyer sawmill with a visible circular saw blade that spun and a lumber cart that moved by the blade.

The No. 364 Lumber Loader reproduction has the stamped-steel construction of the original 1948 version.

Lionel No. 49806 Sawmill re-creates the action of logs going in one side and squared-off lumber coming out the other side.

Lionel's re-creation of the lumber industry on Michael Sadowski's layout (left to right): the No. 14001 Lumber Loader, the No. 49806 Sawmill, and the No. 164 Automated Log Loader.

ACTION LOG CARS

Lionel's log cars are some of the most enjoyable of all of the company's operating cars because they are so fascinating to watch in action. The sight and sound of the tumbling logs (actually wood dowels) has the appearance of an avalanche, but the whole process is well controlled. The coal dump cars may seem like fun, but coal was a mess—logs were clean and simple. At worst, one or two would roll off the layout and under a desk or bed.

Lionel also offered a complete range of logging industry accessories as described on pages 108 and 109. It was the log cars that fed those accessories and, in some cases, were fed by those industries. The Operating Log Car was one of the first four action cars to be produced by Lionel in 1939 (see page 100).

It might seem incongruous to dump logs into one side of an accessory to have them reloaded on the other side, but that was true of coal boxes and with Lionel's other car/accessory pairings. The serious Lionel operators would unload a car and then run the empty car around the layout a few laps to return to some "other" location where the same log loader was used to reload the car with "fresh" logs. The loaded car ran around the layout a few times to dump its load, and the whole process was repeated. The only imagination required was what was happening to the logs in between trips.

Lionel's No. 6361 Log Car used the small steel disc to trigger the unloading mechanism. Modelers often use scale chain to keep the logs in place while the train is moving.

Bill Hitchcock arranged his Lionel No. 364 Log Loader so that the logs are dumped into the loader by railroad car, then loaded into trucks at the lower left.

Lionel offered the No. 3651 stamped-steel Operating Log Car (rear) as one of its first four operating cars in 1939. The post–World War II version (front) has a cast-metal chassis and was introduced in 1947.

THE AUTOMOBILE CARS

The Lionel No. 2758 Automobile Boxcar
had stamped-steel sides and roof die-cast
ends and roof walk.

The real railroads have always played a major role in the distribution of new automobiles. From 1930 to 1960, automobiles often were shipped inside special boxcars with racks to hold two layers of new cars. These boxcars were usually labeled with the word "automobiles" on the outside.

For true Lionel fans, you always have favorite model railroad items, ones that evoke memories of a time long past or of a favorite uncle or your dad. This mundane block of brown-painted metal that mythically transported automobiles is one of those memory-makers for many.

Technically, the automobile car was Lionel's multimaterial boxcar, with stamped-steel sides and roof and die-cast ends and a roof walk. Other Lionel cars used similar production methods, but this was the first one that did not look like a toy. The car was produced in 1941, at a time when Lionel's other freight cars were far more toylike.

The car was one of only a handful of Lionel cars that survived World War II to appear again in the 1945 through 1948 catalogs, when most of the Lionel freight cars had been "upgraded" to injection-molded plastic. Prewar, the cars had stamped-metal trucks and Lionel's quaint box couplers (a hook-and-loop coupler with a box surrounding the hook and loop to force automatic coupling). Postwar, the cars had Lionel's then-new automatic (and massive) knuckle couplers.

But what really made this car click with so many, both now and then, is that it linked the old and new Lionel, the innocence of the pre–World War II era and the hope of the postwar era. It also linked the last days of steam locomotive power with first-generation diesels and marked the beginning of a lifetime of Lionel for many of us. Personally, I was captivated by the photographs of the car in Lionel's 1946 catalog and in *Model Builder* magazines of late 1940s.

And the car was real railroading through and through: the proper color, workaday proportions, and the romantic fantasy that it would carry cars was implied with the word "automobiles" blazoned across the side. The Pennsylvania Railroad herald and name just added mystique that this car was a long way from home.

By the 1960s, full-size automobiles were shipped on open 50-foot flat railroad cars with a rack to hold a second layer of automobiles. Gradually, these flat cars grew to 70 and to nearly 90 feet long, with three racks like the auto racks in use today. Lionel re-created only the earliest of these auto rack cars in 1955. These were replicas of a 40-foot flatcar body that were shorter versions of real railroads' auto loaders, and they have been reproduced many times over the ensuing decades.

Lionel reintroduced the O-27 Auto Rack Car from the 1950s in several paint schemes, including this reproduction of the 1955 original.

A Santa Fe F3ABBA set from 1948 pulls a solid train of Auto Rack Cars on Chris Gans' layout.

O SCALE FREIGHT CARS

Lionel introduced its first accurate-scale model, the incredible replica of the New York Central Hudson, in 1937. Lionel did not, however, produce correct-scale freight cars to match the Hudson until 1940. But when the company did, these freight cars, like the Hudson, were magnificent.

The tank car, hopper, and caboose were made of die-cast metal, and the boxcar was composed of Bakelite or phenolic resin. The molding process allowed Lionel to include intricate rivet detail and grab irons and latches that could not be as well defined with the usual stamped-steel bodies. Like the Hudson, the four freight cars were available as unpainted kits, an indication of how seriously Lionel considered its potential customers to be.

The boxcar had a large single door with a corrugated or "dreadnaught" end and was marked as a Pennsylvania class X-29. The tank car was a single dome of about 10,000-gallon size that was offered lettered for Shell or Sunoco. The hopper was a four-bay offset side lettered for the Baltimore & Ohio, and the caboose was a nice replica of a New York Central wood car lettered for NYC.

The cars survived through World War II in the catalog, but were likely not produced, with sales being filled from prewar inventory. By 1947, only the tank car and hopper

The Lionel O scale freight cars (and the New York Central 4-6-4 Hudson and Pennsylvania 0-6-0 locomotives) were available either assembled or as kits.

appeared in the catalog, but they were gone quickly after that. Lionel reproduced the caboose in injection-molded plastic in 1986.

The O scale tank car was offered lettered for Shell or Sunoco; the hopper was available lettered for the Baltimore & Ohio.

FOUR LAYOUTS FROM THE 1940S

When Lionel started publishing *Model Builder* magazine in the late 1930s, layout drawings were a feature of every issue. Judging by the photographs that Lionel actively solicited for *Model Builder*, there were probably less than a hundred Lionel layouts that looked anything like those illustrations. Most Lionel layouts were just track on a plywood tabletop or a track placed on the floor. The illustrations of these fully finished layouts were either based off of photographs from the 1939 World's Fair layout, from Frank Ellison's layout, or from one of the O scale clubs (most had an outside third rail, rather than Lionel's center rail). Today, scenery techniques have been simplified, and you can buy ready-to-lay grass mats, ground foam for texture, pour-it-in plastic molds, and ready-built buildings, so anyone can have their own exquisite Lionel layout.

The illustrations of those dream Lionel layouts were very detailed, making you feel like you had actually been to this imaginary place. Naturally, the artist included the Lionel accessories that were then currently available. If you look closely, you'll see that most of layouts have stations, signal towers, signals, bridges, and the only operating accessory Lionel offered at that time, the No. 97 Coal Elevator. Some even have the Automatic Crossing Gateman.

Most of these Lionel layouts were illustrated with both an isometric view of the finished layout and a track plan. None of them stipulated the overall size. I have taken an educated guess about the size, based on the assumption that each piece of straight track is about 10 inches long. For the Apartment Railroad layout, I would guess that this was designed to be built with two 4½x5-foot sheets of half-inch plywood, which combined would provide a 5x9-foot space—the size of a ping-pong table.

The A Double-Tracking Plan (from Lionel's 1940 *Handbook for Model Builders*) is divided into electrically isolated blocks with a small dot in the center rail indicating where an insulated track pin would be placed. The plan's "toggle switches" are simply on-off switches. The dashed lines are the connecting wires. The wiring for the uncoupling or unloading tracks is shown, but no wiring for remote-control switches is indicated.

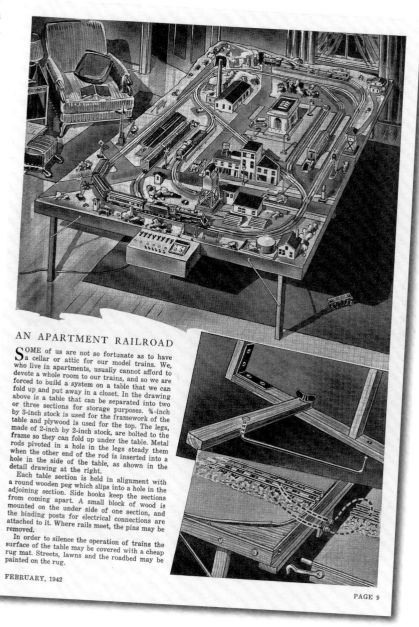

AN APARTMENT RAILROAD

SOME of us are not so fortunate as to have a cellar or attic for our model trains. We, who live in apartments, usually cannot afford to devote a whole room to our trains, and so we are forced to build a system on a table that we can fold up and put away in a closet. In the drawing above is a table that can be separated into two or three sections for storage purposes. ¾-inch by 3-inch stock is used for the framework of the table and plywood is used for the top. The legs, made of 2-inch by 2-inch stock, are bolted to the frame so they can fold up under the table. Metal rods pivoted in a hole in the legs steady them when the other end of the rod is inserted into a hole in the side of the table, as shown in the detail drawing at the right.

Each table section is held in alignment with a round wooden peg which slips into a hole in the adjoining section. Side hooks keep the sections from coming apart. A small block of wood is mounted on the under side of one section, and the binding posts for electrical connections are attached to it. Where rails meet, the pins may be removed.

In order to silence the operation of trains the surface of the table may be covered with a cheap rug mat. Streets, lawns and the roadbed may be painted on the rug.

FEBRUARY, 1942

PAGE 9

The ping-pong-table-size "An Apartment Railroad" layout from the February 1942 issue of *Model Builder*. Lionel's No. 97 Electric Coal Elevator is prominent as is the No. 115 Illuminated Station. Notice that a hopper car has derailed and is lying on the floor—a realistic drawing, to be sure. On these two smaller plans, the No. 155 Illuminated Freight Shed is being used for unloading freight.

"The Railroad Table with a Center Well" layout in the March 1943 issue of *Model Builder* appears to be designed for a 4x8-foot panel on each end with 2x4-foot side pieces for an overall size of 8x12 feet. The No. 97 Electric Coal Elevator is in the upper right with a larger No. 116 Illuminated City Station and two of the stamped-steel No. 315 Illuminated Trestles in the middle left.

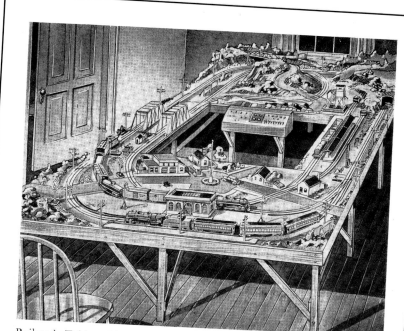

Railroad Table with a Center Well

A big flat-top table may be the easiest type of railroad support to build but it will not accommodate the most interesting and easiest railroad to operate. Illustrated above is a modification of the square table—actually two tables with two ledges extending between them, leaving an open well in the center. In this center area are the remote controls and from this point the operator is able to survey and to reach any part of the line. Notice the construction of a bluff ...he control board.

...construction drawing showing how ...d by the use of green-blue paper ...ndow glass.

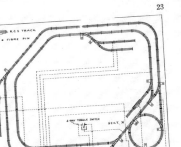

4 PAIRS SWITCHES —17 CURVED SECTIONS
—40 STRAIGHT SECTIONS

PAGE 25

LAYOUT SUGGESTIONS

A DOUBLE-TRACKING PLAN

TWO completely independent loops of track enable trains to be operated without collision. On the outer track a short siding is provided and the inner loop has three side tracks. The plan shows two cross-overs and a reversing circle for either loop.

Power in all the sidings may be cut out. The outside mainline loop is divided into three circuits. The inside loop is likewise divided into three sections but only two large sections are controlled by transformer control No. 1. A double throw toggle switch is provided for the third inner section of track connected to the reversing loop. This is done so that either control No. 1 or No. 2 can energize that section, and train reversing can be controlled by either one of the controllers.

A train running "eastbound" on the outer track can be put into the inner loop. When moving over a train from one loop to the next, the two-way toggle switch is set so that control No. 2 energizes

that section of track. When this switching operation is completed, and the train is on the "westbound" inner track, the two-way toggle switch is again thrown back so that control No. 1 is energizing it.

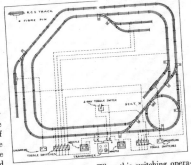

"A Double-Tracking Plan" from page 23 of the *Handbook for Model Builders*, published in 1940, is roughly 12x14 feet. (Railfans refer to parallel tracks as simply "double track.") This one is wired and has electrically isolated blocks so that two trains can operate at once, one on the inner oval, the other on outer oval. The circle in the corner is part of two overlapping reverse loops so that trains can change direction from either oval and from either direction. The tower just to the left of the control panel is Lionel's stamped-steel No. 438 Illuminated Signal Tower. By 1940, when these larger layout plans were first published, Lionel had introduced its long-lived No. 156 Illuminated Station Platform, and one is in the upper right with passenger car parked behind it.

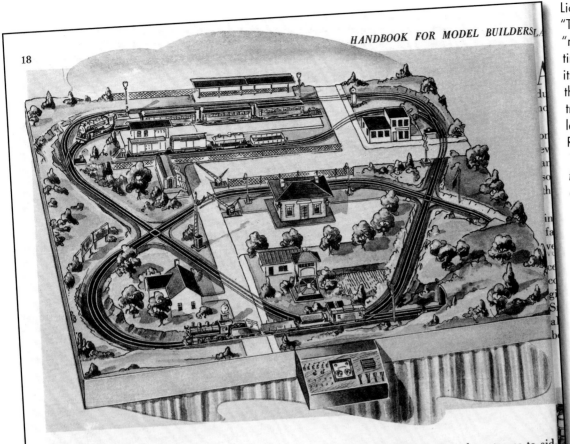

18

Lionel used the word "Trainmaster" (with a small "m" for master) the first time in 1938 to identify its first transformers that would operate two trains at once. This layout, "Small Two-Train Railroad," from page 18 of the *Handbook for Model Builders* was designed to allow one train to switch cars on the upper oval while the second train ran around the lower oval. The depot is the medium-size No. 134 stamped-steel Illuminated Station, and there is no coal elevator. Two No. 156 Illuminated Station Platforms are used to suggest a second town in the upper center with a passenger train parked in front of them. A No. 442 Landscaped Diner is visible just below the two boxcars in the upper left.

SMALL TWO-TRAIN RAILROAD

TWO pairs of switches and two crossings in this layout provide several alternative routes for the passenger and freight train that this system will accommodate.

The two long sidings shown in the layout plan can be used as passing tracks or for the storage of surplus cars.

The layout can be reproduced with "O-27" equipment as easily as with "O" gauge equipment.

A conveniently located control panel box is shown to one side of the railroad table. This houses all the controls.

The track layout is sectionalized, the main line tracks being broken into four sections, each controlled by a toggle switch. The power for either siding can be cut in or out by two other switches.

This sectionalizing is found useful in the operation of two trains, where one is to be stopped for the benefit of the other.

The track diagram calls for the use of three sections of RCS track, located at the entrance to sidings so that a train can back into a siding and uncouple its cars by electric remote control.

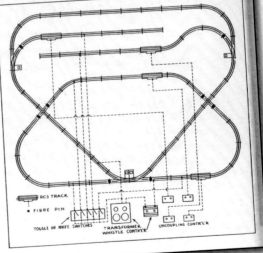

PART IV
THE POSTWAR BOOM

LIONEL'S POSTWAR SURPRISES

While Lionel factories were busy making ship's compasses and other contract products during World War II, the company's designers did not remain idle in coming up with ideas for new products that could be introduced once the war was over. For Christmas of 1945, new trains were ready, and Lionel introduced them in a superb public relations move, delivering the trains right into the hands of handicapped children.

The most exciting feature of these new models was that the steam engines actually smoked. Lionel had spent what today would be several hundred thousand dollars to develop a small pill that, when heated with a wire element similar to that in toasters, produced harmless white smoke. Two years later, in 1949, Lionel developed a pump that delivered the smoke in puffs synchronized with the locomotive's drivers, like the smoke on real steam locomotives. In the late 1940s, the "smoke" pill was replaced by a simpler-to-use fluid.

Lionel also had all-new knuckle-style couplers on the 1945 postwar trains, a feature that most certainly had been developed during the war years because they worked right from that start.

Lionel bounced into the new era with an all-new series of injection-molded plastic cars. The gondola was shipped in 1945, followed by a boxcar, double-dome tank car, and gray work caboose in 1946. In 1947 came a depressed-center flatcar, a single dome tank car, an operating reefer (called a

The exact-scale Pennsylvania Railroad S-1 steam turbine fills the 30-inch turntable on the Lionel Visitor's Center layout.

"milk car"), the Southern Pacific–style caboose, as well as the replica of the heavyweight Pullman car in the Madison series. Smooth-side streamlined passenger cars and a hopper were added in 1948 and a stock car in 1950. Lionel had its first diesel locomotive, a replica of the Electro-Motive

The Pennsylvania Railroad S-2 6-8-6 steam turbine was reintroduced in the mid-1980s as part of the Famous American Railroad Series.

Most Lionel steam locomotives and some diesels have smoke units. Add only three or four drops of Lionel's Smoke Fluid to produce enough smoke for several trips around most layouts.

Corporation's (General Motors) F3A, in 1947. The first operating water tower was another injection-molded plastic product produced in 1948.

For 1946, Lionel had a completely new steam locomotive, its replica of the Pennsylvania Railroad's massive S-2 steam turbine 6-8-6, plastic cars, and operating knuckle couplers. Lionel knew that part of its image centered around that Pennsylvania Railroad S-2 steam locomotive. In 1946 and 1947, the upmarket versions of S-2 were fitted with a 12-wheeled tender from the Scale New York Central Hudson. In 1948, Lionel made the S-2 far more realistic by molding a replica of the full-size locomotive's more-rounded tender. The lowered-price version of S-2 had Lionel's medium-size eight-wheel tender. Even with that massive roundtop tender, however, Lionel's S-2 was only 19 inches long, about two-thirds the size of real thing. Lionel produced a semi-scale replica of the S-2 in 2001, and it is 30 inches long, but should really be a bit longer.

In 1946, Lionel introduced a completely new control system called Electronic Control that used radio frequencies to control the locomotive's whistle, to activate the automatic uncoupling feature, and to allow dump cars to unload anywhere on the track. The system was only available from 1946 to 1949, and nearly all were sold as sets that included the Pennsylvania S-2 Turbine 6-8-6 with a small tender, a Baby Ruth boxcar, a stamped-steel No. 5459 Automatic Dump Car (that dated back to the 1930s), a new plastic gondola, and a new plastic caboose. Each car was fitted with a receiver and Electromagnetic couplers.

Lionel's first post–World War II catalog announced a truly advanced Electronic Control system that used radio frequencies to allow cars to be uncoupled or unloaded anywhere on the track.

PLASTIC FREIGHT CARS

The Work Caboose (right) was one of Lionel's first injection-molded plastic models with toolboxes and body resting on a cast-metal flatcar.

World War II was barely over when plastic appeared on freight car bodies in the Lionel line. At the time, plastic was a wonder material; Americans would not be exposed to the poorly made Japanese toys that made plastic synonymous with cheap for another decade. In 1945, plastic could be used to reproduce fine details like rivet heads, door latches, and panel seams so crisp and clean they looked like separate parts. And there were thousands upon thousands of separate parts on a real freight car, particularly one riveted together from sheet-steel panels. Lionel's plastic car bodies looked like they could actually have been riveted together, too.

Lionel's 1946 catalog included an injection-molded plastic 40-foot boxcar, a two-dome tank car, a gondola, and the superstructure for the work car that was usually coupled beneath the boom of the cast-metal operating crane

car. For reasons I cannot fathom, the boxcar was usually painted orange, lettered with a Pennsylvania Railroad herald and the Baby Ruth candy logo. Lionel's genius was vividly apparent in that car because it evoked a passion in thousands of kids, myself included. It was better than realistic because it featured my favorite candy and included my favorite color on a delightful car with sliding doors and operating knuckle couplers (with the subliminal plus of lettering in chocolate brown).

Lionel added more plastic cars each year in the late 1940s, phasing out what remained of the prewar metal line. The plastic-bodied hopper car and the Southern Pacific–style caboose appeared in 1948, and, with exception of the reproduction stamped-tin cars of the 1930s, Lionel did not return to using metal on freight car bodies.

Lionel's modified the one-piece stock carbody to create the first Operating Cattle Car in 1951.

Lionel produced the first of these injection-molded Southern Pacific cabooses in 1948.

Lionel produced the first one-piece hopper in 1948 and this version with operating bottom hopper doors in 1950.

THE MADISON
PULLMAN CARS

Lionel reintroduced the prewar Madison cars in 1946.

In 1938, Lionel introduced a semi-scale Pullman car to match the New York Central Hudson the company produced in 1937. Before that, Lionel offered train sets that utilized the articulated Milwaukee Road *Hiawatha* cars behind the Hudson. The *Hiawatha* cars were a bit smaller in height and width than the Hudson's tender, but the cars were about 14 inches long. Lionel's semi-scale Pullman also was 14 inches long.

The Lionel model was a replica of the Pullman sleeping cars of the 1930s and 1940s, which were constructed of riveted-together steel. When the streamlined cars appeared in the late 1930s, the earlier cars were referred to as heavyweights. Lionel's replicas of the heavyweight Pullmans were a bit lower and narrower than exact scale, and their length was shortened from true 1/48 scale by about 7 inches. The cars were not made of injection-molded plastic, but formed in a phenolic resin usually called Bakelite.

Lionel provided three versions of the car—the Madison, the Irvington, and the Manhattan—the only difference being

the names on the sides. The cars became known, among Lionel fans, as the Madison cars (which could have stemmed from the name of Lionel's largest and highest-profile dealer, Madison Hardware, in downtown New York).

Lionel reintroduced even shorter versions of the Madison cars in 1973, adding baggage-mail, baggage, diner, and observation cars that the Madison fans from the previous 30 years had been asking for. However, those 1973 cars looked like dwarves beside the semi-scale Madison cars. Lionel reintroduced the Madison cars as 15-inch-long models molded in thicker-than-usual plastic to simulate heft of the 1940s-era Bakelite cars. The 1991 versions kept the same three car names but added a fourth, Sager Place, on the observation car, which was, too obviously, just a Pullman with the end doors replaced by a platform.

Lionel did not fulfill its 1938 promise of a scale Pullman until 2002 when Lionel introduced a fourth, completely new, series of 19-inch-long cars that were correct O scale in width and height but slightly shortened. These top-of-

Lionel introduced shorter versions of the heavyweight Madison-style passenger cars in the 1980s in several paint schemes.

Gino Szymanowski's Alton Railroad passenger train consists of Lionel's semi-scale 4-6-2 Pacific locomotive and 19-inch heavyweight passenger cars.

the-line models even had flexible diaphragms between each car like the prototype, which helped disguise the excess car-to-car gap needed to get the cars around even a 54-inch diameter curve. And this time, Lionel offered a baggage car, a baggage-coach car, a diner, and a correctly proportioned observation car, as well as a Pullman car. Lionel even offered a 50th anniversary set with a semi-scale New York Central Hudson, three Pullmans, and, at last, the baggage and observation car to match. These cars have been offered in a variety of colors and road names, including as a green Santa Fe, a maroon Pennsylvania, a blue-and-gray Baltimore & Ohio, an orange-and-brown Milwaukee, a two-tone orange Southern Pacific, and a red-and-maroon Alton Railroad series of cars.

THE STEAM LOCOMOTIVE WATER TOWER

Lionel's recent reproductions of the No. 30 Water Tower have only the lowering and raising spout action.

The kids of the 1950s knew enough about real railroads to understand that the locomotives that pulled most of the trains developed their power from steam, which was only produced if there was fuel to heat the water. Still, water was as critical as the coal, which is why Lionel came out with the No. 38 Water Tower after World War II. It was one of the first new operating accessories offered in the postwar era.

The tower was a scale model, even if the trains were not. It was also one of first items to be produced in injection-molded plastic, with the legs, tank, and roof all plastic and

The 1950 version of the waterless No. 30 Water Tower is virtually identical to the current reproductions.

a die-cast metal base. At the push of a button, the spout could be lowered over the water hatch on the locomotive's tender. With the No. 38 Water Tower (offered from 1946 to 1948), the magic really began after the spout was lowered. The tank was slightly translucent, so you if you kept the spout down, you could actually watch the water level lower as the locomotive's tender was filled. Over the years, Lionel has continued to produce water towers that looked like No. 38, but the later No. 30 models only had the remote-control water spout.

The real magic of the No. 38 Water Tower was a double-walled tank, so it only needed a few ounces of water. It had a reservoir in the base and a pump that was activated when spout was lowered. The pump moved the water from the tank into the hidden reservoir. The model included small pills of vegetable dye to make the water visible.

Now the No. 38 Water Tower is highly collectible because it was only produced for two years. It was discontinued because the water often leaked, which damaged the metal base. Lionel introduced a modern version of the No. 38 tower in 2001 and, because of its modern materials, it can safely contain the water.

In 2001, Lionel reproduced the No. 38 Water Tower with simulated water-level changes and a raising and lowering spout.

LIONEL'S FIRST DIESEL

Bill Hitchcock has both the Santa Fe and New York Central F3A diesels and the F3B diesels from 1948 and 1949.

The one image of toy trains that nearly everyone recognizes is the reproduction of the Santa Fe's red-and-yellow-nosed silver F3A diesel of the late 1940s. There are probably more than a million of these locomotives as HO, O, S, and N scale models, and they have been reproduced as Christmas ornaments time and time again. Lionel introduced its replicas of the Electro-Motive Division (of General Motors) F3A diesel in 1947, and instantly a million children fell in love.

Lionel pulled out the stops with this locomotive. It had everything the spectacular Pennsylvania GG1 electric locomotive (introduced the previous year) had, including Magne-Traction, dual motors, and Electromagnetic couplers. Those first F3A diesels were offered in either the Santa Fe colors or in New York Central two-tone gray.

The F3A sold as a two-unit set with F3A units back to back. The F3B unit (with no cab on either end) did not appear until 1950. Lionel produced the models until about 1960, but the company also offered less-expensive (and less-detailed) F3A/F3B sets with just a single motor. Lionel produced some even smaller variations of the similar FTA diesel for the entry-level market.

The exact-scale version of the F3A, introduced in 2003, was about 15 percent larger than Lionel's original and, because this one really did fulfill the promise of the paintings in those late-1940s catalogs, it may be the most impressive of all of the locomotives in Lionel's history. This Standard O model was plated to perfectly re-create the appearance of the full-size locomotive's stainless-steel body panels. The model had plenty of power too, with TrainMaster inside. It also had a RailSounds digitally reproduced diesel horn and diesel motor sound and super details like coupler cut levers, windshield wipers, American flags (in place of the white flags the prototype might have carried to indicate another train was following), and, of course, a full interior with engineer and fireman.

The 2003 exact-scale replica of the Santa Fe F3A and F3B diesel is one of Lionel's most realistic diesel locomotives, complete with marker flags and other super details.

LIONEL'S MILK CAR

By 1947, Lionel enthusiasts had become accustomed to the "action" cars that dumped logs, coal, or crates or ejected boxes. Then Lionel produced the unexpected: a workman who actually pushed cans of milk out of a refrigerator car's double doors.

Few of us remember that milk was once delivered by train and often in three-foot high cans, but it was in the early 1900s. By the 1940s, milk delivery by rail was no longer commonplace, but the Association of American Railroads (AAR) still included a milk delivery scene in a series of photographs it distributed to schools across America. So even if the kids did not actually see milkmen in action, the AAR series reminded them of it. Needless to say, Lionel's Milk Car was a hit and, like the other action accessories, its milk cans were moved onto the platform at the push of a button.

Lionel's first series of Milk Cars were relatively small O-27-size models. The Milk Car was upsized in 1955 from 8¾ inches to 10 inches, a match for other Standard O cars but not quite exact 1/48 scale. Lionel temporarily stopped production of the Milk Car in 1966 (one indication of the beginning of Lionel's "dark years"), but production resumed under the Richard Kughn revival in 1985.

Lionel's first Operating Milk Car, offered from 1946 to 1949, was a small O-27-size car.

The mechanism used to allow the workman to push those cans out the door changed only slightly from 1947 to 1985 and is still in use today. The metal milk cans still

The doors on the Operating Milk Car are held shut with hairpin-style springs until the milkman shoves out a can of milk.

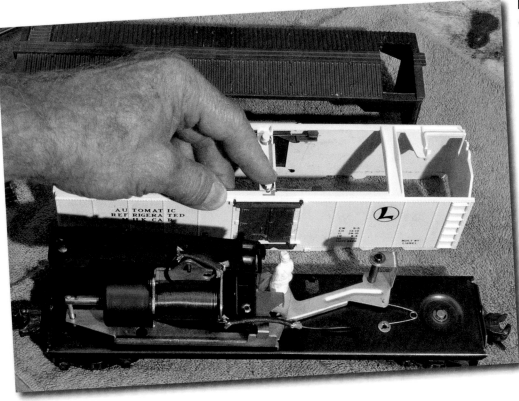

Inside the Operating Milk Car, an electrical solenoid moves the milkman's platform, and the cans are loaded down the chute that directs the cans to the milkman from the rooftop hatch.

In the 1930s and 1940s, milk was delivered by rail to many towns in these large cans. *Photo from the Association of American Railroads*

47. Bringing Milk to the City

Courtesy of U.S.D.A... Photograph by Forsythe

are loaded into the car through a hatch in the roof, and the cans roll down a chute to be dropped onto the floor of the car between the arms of the plastic workman. The workman is mounted on an aluminum platform that pivots out to push the cans onto a steel platform. The cans have small magnets in the base, so they stick to the steel platform until another can pushes them further onto the platform. The effect is quite realistic; you almost expect see that workman to break into sweat.

Lionel never called the car by its proper name, a refrigerator car, or, in railroad talk, a reefer. Lionel has produced a number of different replicas of nonaction reefers, though. In 2003, Lionel also introduced a series of replicas of what really were "milk cars" on the real railroads. These cars, however, did not hold cans of milk; they contained two massive vats inside and, on the outside, they looked like a typical insulated refrigerator car. Technically, these would be milk tank cars, but the tanks are only visible through the open car doors.

Lionel offered this massive No. 408E Standard Gauge electric locomotive with two motors in 1927.

In the Roaring Twenties, the real railroads used locomotives powered by electricity up and down the Northeast corridor and, surprisingly, in the Northwest, too. The Great Northern and the Milwaukee railroads used electric locomotives to surmount the Cascade Mountain range, and the Virginian used electrics over its mountain division in the Appalachians.

For youngsters of that period, there was an obvious link between the massive full-size electric locomotives and a toy model of the same machine. So it was clear to Lionel that the company needed to produce an electric locomotive model, and Lionel's first locomotive was a replica of an electric switching locomotive in 2⅞-inch gauge. When Lionel downsized to Standard Gauge (still massive models with track rails 2⅛ inches between the railheads) in 1906, the first locomotives were 4-4-0 steamers. The first electric, a replica of the New York Central's class S, was introduced in 1910.

The early models were very much compressed replicas, with just four wheels, while the prototype had eight.

Later models were much larger and more accurate, culminating in the 17-inch-long No. 408E of 1927 that had the correct number of wheels, reasonably accurate proportions (these were, after all, tinplate toys), and two massive motors. The first of the O Gauge (1¾ inches between the rails) electric was another condensed replica of the same New York Central locomotive.

Lionel has introduced dozens of re-creations of electric locomotives—from those Pennsylvania S-class engines to the Boston & Maine tunnel engines. However, it was the company's replica of the 1940s-era Pennsylvania Railroad GG1, introduced in 1947, that has become the hallmark Lionel electric. The first Lionel GG1s had a single motor and horn actuated by a vibrator. In 1955, the model was upgraded with two motors, Magne-Traction, and Electromagnetic couplers. All of these GG1 models, at just 14 inches long, were compressed versions of the prototype. Lionel produced a Standard O GG1 in 2004 that was close to exact scale and was 20 inches long.

Lionel's first replica of the GG1 from 1947 on Bill Hitchcock's layout.

Chris Gans has collected all the significant variations of the GG1s Lionel produced from 1947 to 1969. Lionel produced several more varieties in the past two decades, to match most of these.

LIONEL'S 50TH YEAR

Lionel was mounting success upon success in 1950, in the midst of the company's largest sales and largest profit years. Lionel's big surprise for its 50th anniversary was that it would provide all its O Gauge locomotives with more pulling power by providing more traction between drivers or wheels and the rails. This would be accomplished through the "magic" of Magne-Traction.

Lionel had been using powdered metal to cast wheels and driver tires for years, and this powdered or "sintered" metal could be molded much like plastic—with a slick surface that seldom required machining. Lionel experimented and discovered that it could use magnetized particles in the metal alloy, so the driver tires on steam locomotives and the wheels on diesel locomotives would be magnetic.

Since Lionel's track rails were steel, the magnetic driver and wheels would provide more traction and less slip, so any existing model could pull more cars up steeper grades. Magne-Traction sounded fantastic to young Lionel fans, even though many of them did not have enough cars to tax the pulling power of the locomotives with or without Magne-Traction.

For me, the most exciting part of Lionel's 50th anniversary celebration was the introduction of the company's replica of the 1950 Union Pacific–decorated Alco FA-2 diesel to pull the smooth-side streamlined cars introduced in 1948. This was the first Lionel streamlined passenger train since the *M10000* and the *Zephyr* of 1934 and 1935. The Alco FA-2 was at least as gorgeous as the EMD F3A.

Lionel's F2A, however, was a much smaller locomotive, more O-27 than O Gauge, and the body sat high above the trucks, so it did not capture the proportions of the prototype nearly as well as Lionel's replica of the Electro-Motive Corporation F3A. Regardless, this was Lionel's first post–World War II replica of a streamlined passenger train, and while you couldn't see Magne-Traction, you sure could see the bright yellow-and-gray red-striped streamliner.

Lionel displayed a leap of faith by not offering a single steam locomotive in its 1951 catalog. Presumably, you already had all the steam locomotives you wanted or, if not, you could buy one of nine train sets. Yet, you could have any diesel the company made, and the practice of only listing diesels for separate sale continued through the 1950s.

Lionel reproduced its 1950 pair of FA-2 diesels in 1994.

Lionel offered the FA-2 in silver in 1951, a color the Union Pacific never used, but it proved popular with Lionel fans.

A pair of Union Pacific Alco FA-2s with matching smooth-side cars from 1994 on the Lionel Visitor's Center layout.

LIONEL'S 1940s STREAMLINERS

Lionel's first smooth-side cars, from 1948, on Gil Bruck's layout.

Lionel created new model railroad dreams for boys and girls each year in the late 1940s and, for 1948, Lionel offered them its first replicas of the streamlined, smooth-side passenger cars that were then common on all the real railroads.

Those were the days when Lionel's catalogs were illustrated with paintings, so it was not obvious that these new cars were shorter than the real thing—a lot shorter. When the cars actually appeared, they were illustrated as part of the 2140WS De Luxe Passenger Set pulled by the massive replica of the Pennsylvania Railroad's S-2 6-8-6 steam turbine, and they looked magnificent. When the cars were produced, however, they looked a lot shorter than the real thing and sat high on their trucks.

They were part of Lionel's deluxe line at first, but in the 1980s, when Lionel started producing Standard O passenger cars with extruded aluminum bodies that were the correct height and width, the original smooth-side cars were downgraded to the O-27 entry-level line.

Lionel's smooth-side cars of the 1940s were only 12 inches long, while the later extruded-aluminum replicas of

the real railroads' stainless-steel corrugated cars of 1952 were 19 inches long (and they should have been 2 inches longer). Nevertheless, thousands of children wanted those smooth-side cars.

Lionel elected to paint the first series of these 12-inch smooth-side cars an odd shade of apple green with yellow stripes that matched no know real railroad paint scheme—and, perhaps, that was the company's goal. In 1950, Lionel offered them in Union Pacific yellow and gray with red stripes and in silver. All three color options retained the "Lionel Lines" lettering above the windows.

Like the Madison replicas of the heavyweight Pullman cars, Lionel named each of these 12-inch streamliners. The two green or silver coaches were Chatham and Maplewood, and the green or silver observation car was Hillside. The yellow cars were known as either Plainfield, Westfield, or Livingston. Lionel produces the cars today and has offered them in number of different paint schemes, including New York Central two-tone gray.

In 1951, Lionel offered the three-car Union Pacific streamliner in silver, rather than yellow and gray.

Lionel's current 12-inch extruded-aluminum smooth-side cars are much shorter than the prototype but accurate O scale in width and length.

LIONEL DIESELIZES

By the mid-1950s, nearly all of the major railroads had converted from steam locomotives to diesels. Lionel introduced its incredible replicas of the Electro-Motive Division (of General Motors) F3A diesel in 1948. The cab-less F3B appeared in 1950.

In 1949, Lionel introduced its replica of EMD's NW2 eight-wheeled diesel switcher. The next year, Lionel offered replicas of the Alco FA-2 diesels in Union Pacific yellow and gray.

Lionel hoped it had a locomotive to match the popularity of the F3A when the massive 17-inch-long, 12-wheeled replica of the Fairbanks-Morse TrainMaster came out in 1954 with two motors and Magne-Traction.

Lionel's replica of the then-common Electro-Motive Division GP7 appeared in 1955, and the ungainly double-ended General Electric 44-ton diesel appeared in 1956. The Lionel replica of the EMD GP9 (nearly identical to the GP7, except for bulges on the sides of the high hood house the dynamic brake cooling on the full-size locomotives) was launched in 1958, with GP7 appearing later. That diesel roster was expanded considerably with dozens of alternate paint schemes, but those eight basic models were the only ones in the Lionel lineup until 1970.

Lionel's 2005 version of the GP9 diesel.

Railfans refer to the diesels that were produced before about 1965 as first-generation models, a term that applies to all of these early Lionel diesels. In the 1980s, Lionel began to add a long series of "second generation" diesels and replicas of the most modern diesels to its roster of available models.

Lionel's first replica of the Electro-Motive Division's NW2 diesel switcher in 1949 was lettered for the Santa Fe like this unit on Ralph Johnson's layout.

The Fairbanks-Morse TrainMaster diesel was reintroduced by Lionel in the mid-1980s. This is the 2002 version.

The General Electric 44-ton diesel was introduced in 1957. This is the 44-tonner reintroduced in 1993 on the Lionel Visitor's Center layout.

THE LIONELVILLE STATION

Lionel's *Polar Express* is just entering the tunnel opposite a No. 133 Lighted Passenger Station on Lester Kushner's layout at Main Line Hobbies in East Norristown, Pennsylvania.

Lionel was quick to adopt the name "Lionelville" for its passenger stations, with the name appearing on several versions of the company's stamped-steel stations in 1923. Over the years, the name appeared on a variety of both stamped-steel and plastic stations. Recently, Lionel has applied the term to an entire town with ready-built stores, houses, and playground equipment and, of course, passenger stations.

Lionel's first injection-molded plastic model station, the No. 132 with an automatic train-stopping and starting feature, was offered in 1949 with "Lionelville" appearing on the placards on the station's eaves. Lionel had offered an automatic train stopper circuit in its stamped-steel Lionel City Station in 1936, but it was dropped from the Lionel line

in 1950. In the early 1970s, Lionel offered the same station and called it a freight station, but the only action was interior lighting. Lionel's "small station" replacement included the automatic train-stopping and starting circuit.

The newsstand was a natural addition to any Lionel station. Lionel provided both nonanimated and animated newsstands, both introduced in 1957 and reproduced several times. The No. 114 Newsstand had a built-in diesel horn, and the No. 118 Newsstand had a built-in whistle. Both were controlled by a remote-controlled push button. The No. 128 Animated Newsstand was also introduced in 1957, with a news dealer who moves and a boy whose puppy runs around a hydrant, again, at the push of a button.

Lester Kushner positioned a Lionel Newsstand with Horn beside a No. 133 Lighted Passenger Station.

Lionel's No. 132 Operating Passenger Station (left) and the stamped-steel No. 112 Metropolitan Station.

CATTLE CARS

Lionel offered stamped-steel stock cars in the 1930s. However, it was not until 1950 that the company produced its first injection-molded stock car, with details to match Lionel's other postwar plastic cars. If it was an action car, Lionel called it a "cattle car." But if only the doors opened, it was a "stock car."

Lionel's engineers couldn't figure out how to get cattle in and out of the same door. They solved the problem by fitting two doors, one near each end, so the cattle entered though the right door and exited through the left. It was up to the operator to decide when the car was loaded. The trick was to get as many of the cattle as possible nose to tail, then let up on the button when the first loaded cow began to peek out the left door. The platform was stamped steel and included three aisles with gates that could be opened by hand. This allowed the cows to line up in the least possible space.

The Operating Cattle Car was very similar to the non-operating version in its details; in fact, the opposite side from the loading doors was nearly identical. The cattle car was later offered in two different operating versions—one with opening doors in each end of one side, the other with a hole in each end of the roof for figures or animals to pop in and out. Like the Operating Milk Car, the Operating Cattle Car was something that children of the 1950s could better understand than the coal- or log-loading accessories.

Lionel produced another variation of the Operating Cattle Car in 1956 called the operating horse car. The loading and unloading principle was the same, but the corral for the horses was at tabletop level, with ramps leading up to the two doors on the ends of the side.

Another version of the stock car appeared in 1956 as the No. 3356 Operating Horse Car and Corral with a labyrinth for the horses so that they could stay in line for reloading.

PUMPING OIL

Michael Ulewicz grouped oil derricks and an oil pumping station to create this oil industry scene.

It is easy enough to see coal or logs being dumped, but seeing fluid in motion is a bit more difficult to reproduce on a floor or tabletop. Lionel accomplished that spectacularly with the No. 38 Water Tower (see page 127), using a semi-transparent tank and colored water that actually did lower the water level as it was magically "pumped" into the locomotive tender.

Showing oil being pumped was a bit more difficult. Lionel opted for an orange fluid being visibly "pumped" through clear pipes. The fluid-in-motion effect was achieved with bubbles. The "oil" in the pumping oil derrick was a colored fluid that bubbled when hot, much like that used in the classic Christmas tree bubble lights of the 1940s and 1950s. Lionel's oil-pumping mechanism, the No. 455 Oil Derrick, was introduced in 1954. The pump arm moved up and down in the rocking motion while oil bubbled through a 3-inch-long clear plastic pipe.

Lionel also offered the gas-flow-simulating bubble tubes in its No. 24112 Oil Field with Bubble Tubes in 2003.

Lionel reproduced the Operating Fueling Station in 1993.

The company's No. 415 Diesel Fueling Station, introduced in 1955, included a workman who automatically came out of his shed when the oil-delivery pipe was pivoted over the locomotive—all at the push of a button. Lionel fans often position this diesel fueling station near the oil derrick to make it a bit more obvious what is coming out of the oil depot's delivery pipe.

YOUR HAND ON
THE THROTTLE

Oliver Gaddini has two Lionel ZW transformers wired to allow the use of either them or TrainMaster Command Control. The green switches are Atlas and turn electrical blocks on or off.

During the first half of the twentieth century, electricity was still accepted as a kind of magic that could perform tasks no one could have imagined possible. Lionel trains operated by electricity and, by implication, were themselves a form of magic. What made it all come to life, though, was that you could control that magic. The controls were located on a box called a transformer.

The term "transformer" was a reasonably accurate description of what went on inside the box where a 115-volt AC household current was reduced to about 20 volts to render it relatively harmless. The toy train transformer carried more than just the means of reducing the voltage, though. The transformer also contained a speed control, a reversing switch and, in some cases, a horn button.

Most of Lionel's locomotives have a truly peculiar electronic device called an E-unit connected to the motor. The E-unit was turned on and off whenever the power to rails was turned on and off. However, each time the E-unit was turned on, it either reversed the current to the motor, turned the

current off, or reversed the current again. If the locomotive was sitting on the track and you turned on the power, the locomotive usually just sat there. If you pushed the on-off button on the transformer, the E-unit would flick to either forward or in reverse, and the locomotive would move. If the locomotive was not going the way you desired, you pushed the on-off button once more, and the locomotive would stop. If you pushed the button again, the locomotive would move off in the opposite direction of when you started this sequence. It all sounds absolutely mad, but Lionel fans got used it.

Lionel still uses a similar circuit in the majority of its locomotives. On some of the lowest-priced locomotives, the E-unit is just a small metal lever in front of the cab that must be moved by hand to reverse the locomotive.

Most of Lionel's' small- to medium-size transformers had a simple knob or a short lever that was moved to control speed. The largest Lionel transformers had four knobs and could control two trains (on two separate tracks)—the

Three vintage ZWs and one modern ZW, with 39 control levers for the switches, run the trains and other accessories on David Seebach's layout.

second pair of knobs was used to control power to lights on accessories, the third and forth knobs allowed you to turn lights up or down or speed up or slow down the rate at which logs were being carried up the log loader or coal up the coal elevator.

In 1948, Lionel introduced the most amazing transformer in the history of toy trains, the TrainMaster ZW (by perhaps not a so odd coincidence, Lionel's 1995 digital system was also called TrainMaster but with a capital "M"). The 1948 transformer commonly referred to as the ZW did not survive Lionel's bleak period. It was dropped from the

line in 1954. However, it was so popular that Lionel re-created it (with the need for two external power sources) in 1992, and it survives today.

The original ZW had two massive knobs, each with a concentric ring. The outer knob also had a lever and was used to control two trains. The two inside rings could be used to set the speed for two more trains; yes, the ZW could run four trains at once, all on separate tracks. Independent control of four trains on the same track (without the need for electrically isolated blocks) had to wait for TrainMaster Command Control in 1995.

HOBOES, COPS, AND POP-UPS

During the steam era of real railroading, the concept of hopping on a freight train to get a free ride to parts unknown became a romantic fantasy for millions of boys. The idea of hitching a free ride was, of course, illegal, and the railroads hired professional policemen to keep the free riders or hoboes off the freights. So in its quest for realism, Lionel over the years produced a series of "action" freight cars depicting the chase scenes between cop and hobo.

One of the strangest hobo and cop cars produced was Lionel's No. 3557 Hydraulic Platform Maintenance Car, introduced in the 1950s. The car had an odd gray platform on the top and was supplied with a bridge. You positioned one of figures (cop or hobo) on the top the car, the other on top of the bridge. The platform was spring-loaded to extend about 1½ inches above the car, far enough so that it would rub the bottom of the special bridge. As the car rolled

beneath the bridge, one figure would be pried off the roof to land on the bridge while the figure on the bridge landed on the top of the car. A much simpler version was produced in 1995, with a trackside platform for a boxcar with hobo and cop figures.

Another Lionel cop-chasing-a-hobo car was a gondola with a motorized conveyor that moved a cop and a hobo figure around and around a stack of crates in the center of the car. This one was introduced in 1957, came back in 1980, and was offered again in 1995.

Lionel has offered dozens of animated stock cars and boxcars where figures pop up from the car. In these, a figure pops in and out of a hatch (or two) on the roof or side of the car as the car rolls along. Beneath the car is a lever, which moves up and down as a result of an eccentric cam on one of the axles. When the lever moves up, the figure pops out.

The No. 3557 Hydraulic Platform Maintenance Car.

The 1995 version of Lionel's cop-chasing-the-hobo gondola.

The pop-up Bugs Bunny and Yosemite Sam stock car and rhinoceros boxcar.

The gunfight car used the pop-up levers to move two cowboys with pistols in and out of two openings in the side of a special stock car. This one was furnished with the 1880-era sets. Lionel also has a similar stock car where the dueling cowboys pop in and out of holes in the roof.

PLASTIC TOY TRAINS

Lionel's entry-level cars include the unpainted sliding-door boxcar, 6045 Series Double-Dome Tank Car, and SP-style caboose.

This is Lionel's "cheap stuff," the freight cars that were nearly free if you mailed in cereal or soup coupons and the cars that were promotional items in gasoline stations and hardware stores. Some of these Lionel plastic boxcars even did double duty as banks, with a slot for coins in the roof and removable bodies. These were part of Lionel's method of getting several hundred thousand train sets into the marketplace and of promoting the hobby in general.

The cars were introduced in 1958, and most are still being produced with newer dies. These were the cars that kept Lionel alive (but barely) through 1960s when General Mills took over the line. To the hobby industry, these low-cost items are sold under the category of promotional trains, yet surprisingly, in many cases, these promotional cars and train sets are the most collectible and valuable of all of Lionel's post–World War II production. Often, an odd batch of these was produced, making a few hundred slightly different cars that now collectors clamor for.

The best-selling Lionel car of all time was among these low-priced plastic cars: the 8¼-inch-long 6014 Series boxcar with double doors. It was a one-piece body with molded-on doors, a metal floor, and other details. The bodies all had the same proportions, and the cars were originally fitted with a magnetically operated coupler on both ends. However, in the 1960s, only one operating coupler was installed with a fixed or "dummy" coupler on the opposite end. Lionel sold conversion couplers for these cars if you wanted automatics on both ends. The cars were included in nearly all the lowest-cost train sets. Lionel also offered a slightly upmarket version of the unpainted plastic boxcar with a sliding door.

Lionel had a few other one-piece cars in the lineup to fill out the entry-level and promotional train sets, including a 6142 Series Gondola, a 6045 Series Double-Dome Tank Car, and a caboose.

The SP-style caboose had a magnetic coupler on one end, but no coupler on the other. The cheapest of the cabooses had no end platforms, while slightly more-expensive versions had just end railings. The best ones had both end railings and ladders. Some of the cabooses had separate smoke jacks, while others just had a flat spot on the roof. The SP-style caboose was a typically shortened and shrunk version of the Southern Pacific's standard steel caboose of the 1940s. It was Lionel's first plastic caboose in 1948, and the higher-quality originals came equipped with simulated tool boxes on the underframe, a metal smokestack, interior lights, and electromagnetic couplers on both ends, and those upmarket cars also were painted.

The lower-cost Lionel cars have used two types of automatic couplers, both actuated by the electromagnet in the Uncoupling Track. The early cars had a manual uncoupling tab on the top of the coupler (right), and later cars have the tab on the bottom right side of the coupler.

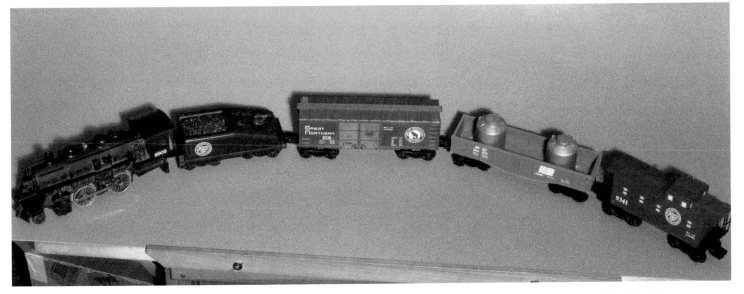

This set was typical of Lionel's entry-level product line in 1979, with a 2-4-0 locomotive, the one-piece double-door boxcar, gondola, and SP-style caboose.

ACTION INDUSTRIES

Ever on the lookout for another industry to replicate for a model railroad layout, Lionel inventor Richard G. Smith (the man also credited with creating Lionel's Operating Milk Car) devised the culvert or pipe loader and unloader in 1956, complete with a special gondola. This accessory actually is two pieces, the No. 342 Culvert Loader and No. 345 Culvert Unloading Station, with a third, the No. 6342 Gondola, also included.

The unloading station positions a magnet over the car to pick up the steel tube culverts and deposit them on the ramp. The culverts then roll down to the loading station. Here, another magnet and crane lifts the steel culverts from the ramp and swings them into the waiting gondola.

The No. 362 Barrel Loaders, introduced in 1952, were far simpler devices. The barrels were dumped from a special gondola into a waiting bin; then a conveyor hoisted them up to a bin with a gate. When the button was pushed, the gate opened, and the barrels were dumped into another waiting gondola.

An electromagnet is energized to pick up the steel culverts from the No. 342 Culvert Loader, and it is released to drop them into a waiting gondola.

The No. 342 Culvert Loader and the No. 345 Culvert Unloading Station on Bill Hitchcock's layout.

An original No. 362 Barrel Loader placed back to back with the unloading platform for the Automatic Milk Car on Bill Hitchcock's layout.

The Barrel Loader is used with a special gondola with a center trough to position the barrels in line for more reliable unloading.

LIONEL'S 1800s-ERA TRAINS

The locomotive is Lionel's 1860-era Virginia & Truckee 4-4-0 with a similar-era combine and coach.

Lionel offered the 4-4-0 in bright brass plate to simulate gold from the Golden Arrow set.

While Lionel has been around more than 100 years, its beginning was not when railroads were first built in the United States. Nevertheless, the company eventually wanted to re-create some of those 1800s-era locomotives and cars, and it finally did so in 1977 with a replica of the Civil War–era Western & Atlantic Railroad *General*.

The *General* had four pilot wheels and four drivers, a 4-4-0. These 4-4-0 locomotives were also called Americans, and thousands were produced with very similar appearance from 1850 to 1890. Lionel also offered the model painted to match one of those used on the real Virginia & Truckee Railroad, the *Reno* (which was part of the 20th Century Fox full-size prop department in the 1950s and 1960s).

In addition, Lionel has offered the 4-4-0 as the Circus Railroad locomotive, painted to match the Disneyland Railroad; as a Union Pacific version with brass-plated boiler; a red-and-maroon Santa Fe version; and a half dozen others. A gray Confederate locomotive and train and a matching blue Union one were offered as a Civil War set in 1999.

Lionel also created an 1860-era truss rod underframe coach and baggage mail car, as well as a similar stock car, boxcar, and flatcar.

Lionel's 2007 replica of the 1830 *Best Friend of Charleston* was hand-made from soldered-together brass pieces, then painted and decorated.

Recently, Lionel has introduced a new series of historical locomotives that includes the *Best Friend of Charleston* from 1830 and the *John Bull* from 1831.

Lionel's James Gang set was introduced in 1980 and included a flatcar, stock car, and mail car patterned after 1880-era cars.

THE SPACE AGE

The United States was enthralled with the space race in 1958 when Lionel introduced the No. 175 Rocket Launcher.

Lionel has been ever alert to what its young customers might crave. During the 1950s space race craze, Lionel introduced the No. 175 Rocket Launcher, an accessory that has been reproduced several times.

The No. 6175 Flat Car was an ancillary part of the launcher because it was designed to carry the rocket, (usually a red-and-white "U.S. Navy" ICBM—intercontinental ballistic missile).

Here is how the accessory works: The rocket has a magnet in the end, so the crane on the rocket launcher can lift the rocket, then roll down the gantry tracks to position the rocket on the launch pad. A rocket launching tower with a motorized gantry moved the rocket launch pad and had a control panel complete with countdown and launch button. The rocket was not the *Apollo*, though, rather a war-headed ICBM. Lionel also offered gondolas with ready-to-launch missiles and flatcar loads of additional missiles in the 1950s.

To complement the ICBM, Lionel also offered its radioactive waste flatcar with containers and flatcars with loads of a condenser and heat exchanger destined for a new atomic plant (or for creating bombs at the notorious Rocky Flats Plant in Colorado). And Lionel offered its own nuclear reactor in 2000. The "reactor" is actually a chrome-plated sphere where an arm picks up the fresh "fuel" (small ball bearings) and moves it inside. Another set of glow-in-the-dark bearings is housed inside, and they are dumped into the waiting car. It's up to you (the operator) to replace the shiny steel ball bearings with round pieces of spent fuel (not really nuclear waste, thankfully, rather just glow-in-the-dark balls).

Lionel's 2001 reproduction of the No. 175 Rocket Launcher beside a No. 264 Operating Forklift Platform on Lester Kushner's layout.

Perhaps the most eclectic Lionel accessory ever, the Nuclear Reactor with glow-in-the-dark fuel pellets on Oliver Gaddini's layout.

THE LIONEL LINES RAILROAD

Lionel created the Phantom III locomotive and articulated passenger cars as a fantasy series of what its designers imagined trains of the future would look like back in 1920.

For many Lionel fans, the model railroad hobby is all about Lionel trains, not much more. These Lionel fans have only a passing interest in the real railroad equipment Lionel has re-created. For them, the Lionel world has only an occasional New York Central or Amtrak locomotive passing through. Their interest lies in what Lionel makes, not what inspired the company's products.

And Lionel became the legendary company it is thanks to those enthusiasts. Lionel did use real-railroad prototype cars and locomotives as its inspiration in the early years, making its products at the time instantly recognizable to longtime railfans. Yet in the late 1930s, Lionel began offering not only replicas of specific real railroad locomotives and cars, but also pure and simple toys.

Many of these products were labeled as a part of Lionel Lines, an imaginary railroad that now has become a long-honored tradition.

Lionel knows its Lionel Lines trains are not taken seriously by all its customers, so over the years these trains have been offered in some strange paint schemes. For example, around 1999 a blue-and-yellow-flamed GP9 appeared with a matching observation car and two flatcars, one with a flame-painted pickup truck, the other with a flame-painted dragster. These were part of The Custom Series set (without track).

Lionel boldly created its own train prototypes in 1999 with the Pratt's Hollow four-car passenger train and locomotive, styled to suggest something from another planet. Lionel reintroduced these pieces with three different color schemes as the Phantom I, Phantom II, and Phantom III from 2000 to 2002. Lionel was back again in 2008 with a fourth color scheme known as the Phantom IV.

Lionel offered a complete train decorated with these hot rod racing flames in 1999.

The Lionel medium-size 4-6-2 Pacific steam locomotive was offered in bright blue, orange, and ivory Lionel colors to become an instant collector's item.

Lionel produced a Centennial Series that included this SD40 with two motors, RailSounds, and Magne-Traction (from the Mizell Trains collection in Westminster, Colorado).

Lionel also offered a set of four matching tank cars and a caboose for the 1999 Centennial Series.

LIONEL'S CONSTRUCTION SETS

The pages of the instruction manual for the Lionel Construction Set included this Operating Draw Bridge (more accurately, a lift bridge), similar to the ones Lionel would produce more than 50 years later.

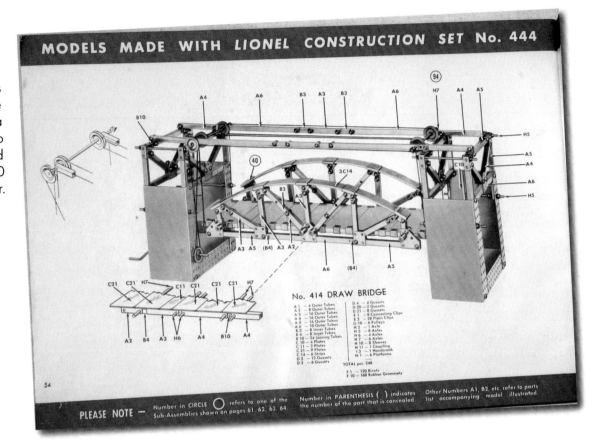

MODELS MADE WITH *LIONEL* CONSTRUCTION SET No. 444

No. 414 DRAW BRIDGE

A 1 — 4 Outer Tubes	D 4 — 4 Gussets
A 2 — 8 Outer Tubes	D 20 — 2 Gussets
A 3 — 16 Outer Tubes	D 21 — 8 Gussets
A 4 — 16 Outer Tubes	E 1 — 8 Connecting Clips
A 5 — 16 Outer Tubes	E 3 — 28 Plain Clips
A 6 — 10 Outer Tubes	G 10 — 6 Pulleys
B 3 — 8 Inner Tubes	H 2 — 1 Axle
B 4 — 8 Inner Tubes	H 5 — 8 Axles
B 10 — 24 Joining Tubes	H 6 — 6 Axles
C 10 — 4 Plates	H 7 — 6 Axles
C 21 — 2 Plates	H 10 — 8 Sheves
C 21 — 9 Plates	H 11 — 1 Coupling
C 14 — 6 Strips	13 — 1 Handcrank
D 2 — 12 Gussets	N 1 — 6 Platforms
D 3 — 6 Gussets	

TOTAL pcs. 240

F 1 — 120 Rivets
F 10 — 160 Rubber Grommets

PLEASE NOTE — Number in CIRCLE ◯ refers to one of the Sub-Assemblies shown on pages 61, 62, 63, 64. Number in PARENTHESIS ( ) indicates the number of the part that is concealed. Other Numbers A1, B2, etc. refer to parts list accompanying model illustrated.

Today, Lionel exclusively focuses on producing trains, both for toy lovers and hobbyists, but over the years some of the toy products Lionel has produced have included chemistry sets and construction sets. It was certainly no coincidence that Lionel's major competitor in the toy train market, American Flyer, was also the source of a very successful series of chemistry sets, Erector Sets, and Mysto Magic sets, all produced by American Flyer's parent company, A. C. Gilbert.

Chemistry experiments were fascinating to teenagers in the 1940s, part of the reason why Lionel introduced its Chem-Lab series of chemistry sets in 1941. These five sets ranged from a small box of about 10 chemicals, tweezers, test tubes, and a manual to the massive set with nearly 50 different chemicals, a balance scale, a Bunsen burner, a half-dozen test tubes, and other equipment. Like the Daisy BB Air Rifle of this same period, some parents (like mine!) wouldn't let their kids fool with either chemical experiments or rifles. (This may be why Lionel included the Chem-Lab in its 1947 train catalog, but it never appeared again.)

On the other hand, the Erector Set was one of more popular toys among parents and kids. It included hundreds of stamped-steel girders and beams, nuts and bolts, and either clockwork or electric motors. From these, you could assemble an endless array of bridges, Ferris wheels, automobiles and trucks, simulated steam engines, and more. Many kids built bridges and other accessories for their Lionel trains from Erector Set parts.

So developing an Erector-type set was a no-brainer for Lionel. Lionel introduced its series of construction sets in 1947. Lionel's set used aluminum tube and sheet for parts, while the Erector Set's were all steel. The Erector Set used nuts and slotted-head screws to assemble the joints and included both a wrench and screwdriver so that you could tighten them down. Lionel took the "rivet" approach to assembly, something that could be advertised as being more typical of construction than mere screws.

Traditional rivets are secured by heating the plain end hot enough so that it can be hammered over for an incredibly tight joint. Obviously, Lionel could not have kids melting metal, so the company used rivets but with rubber washers to hold the rivet in place. It was a poor choice because the rubber washers were just not a tight enough fit. As a result of the poor design, Lionel dropped the construction set from the catalog in 1949.

MODELS MADE WITH LIONEL CONSTRUCTION SET No. 444

No. 406
FERRIS WHEEL

A 1 — 16 Outer Tubes
A 3 — 16 Outer Tubes
A 4 — 16 Outer Tubes
A 5 — 16 Outer Tubes
A 6 — 16 Outer Tubes
B 3 — 4 Inner Tubes
B 4 — 8 Inner Tubes
B 10 — 32 Joining Tubes
C 10 — 8 Plates
C 14 — 16 Strips
C 20 — 8 Plates
D 1 — 16 Gussets
D 2 — 8 Gussets
D 20 — 16 Gussets
E 3 — 40 Plain Clips
G 2 — 6 Hubs
H 2 — 8 Axles
H 3 — 8 Axles
H 5 — 6 Axles
H 6 — 6 Axles
H 7 — 4 Axles
H 10 — 4 Sleeves
H 11 — 3 Couplings
N 1 — 4 Platforms
N 2 — 8 Platform Fittings

TOTAL pcs. 291

F 1 — 88 Rivets
F 10 — 160 Rubber Grommets

AT THIS END OF A6
INSERT B10 WITH
TWO HOLES SHOWING

THESE TUBES CONNECTED
BY CLIPS E3 AND PLATES

PLEASE NOTE — Number in CIRCLE ◯ refers to one of the Sub-Assemblies shown on pages 61, 62, 63, 64. Number in PARENTHESIS ( ) indicates the number of the part that is concealed. Other Numbers A1, B2, etc. refer to parts list accompanying model illustrated.

The icon of the steel Erector Set was a Ferris wheel, so Lionel illustrated how to build one with the its Construction Set.

MODELS MADE WITH LIONEL CONSTRUCTION SET No. 444

No. 404
BASCULE
BRIDGE

A 1 — 14 Outer Tubes
A 2 — 10 Outer Tubes
A 3 — 4 Outer Tubes
A 4 — 16 Outer Tubes
A 5 — 4 Outer Tubes
A 6 — 8 Outer Tubes
B 3 — 8 Inner Tubes
B 10 — 32 Joining Tubes
C 10 — 3 Plates
C 11 — 4 Plates
C 14 — 8 Strips
C 23 — 2 Plates
D 1 — 4 Gussets
D 2 — 4 Gussets
D 3 — 2 Gussets
D 10 — 4 Gussets
D 20 — 8 Gussets
D 23 — 8 Gussets
E 1 — 2 Connecting Clips
E 3 — 8 Plain Clips
G 10 — 1 Pulley
H 4 — 1 Axle
H 3 — 3 Axles
H 6 — 6 Axles
H 7 — 6 Axles
H 10 — 8 Sleeves
H 11 — 4 Couplings
J 3 — 1 Handcrank
N 1 — 6 Platforms

TOTAL pcs. 183

F 1 — 106 Rivets
F 10 — 160 Rubber Grommets

The manual in the larger Lionel Construction Set provided the information to assemble this Bascule Bridge.

PLEASE NOTE — Number in CIRCLE ◯ refers to one of the Sub-Assemblies shown on pages 61, 62, 63, 64. Number in PARENTHESIS ( ) indicates the number of the part that is concealed. Other Numbers A1, B2, etc. refer to parts list accompanying model illustrated.

This is the No. 2153WS Four-Car Deluxe Work Train (with smoke and whistle) from page 18 of Lionel's 1949 catalog.

Most Lionel fans spent endless hours staring at Lionel's catalogs, imagining those trains in their bedroom, basement, or attic. As adults, a few of us have been able to create a time warp by actually building one of the Lionel layouts we fantasized about from the catalogs or from *Model Builder* magazine or Lionel's books. Another of those time warp thrills that Lionel railroaders can create is to assemble the train sets they wanted as a child. Invariably, they'll add a car or two to upgrade the set, just as they did in their imaginations with that Lionel catalog in hand.

Bill Hitchcock has collected virtually every locomotive, every car, and every accessory Lionel offered in the 1947 to 1955 period. He can, then, open any of those catalogs and assemble any train set Lionel made. He built shelves to hold all the locomotives and cars and a model railroad large enough to operate the trains in appropriate Lionel-esque scenery, complete with all the operating accessories from those same catalogs.

Bill Hitchcock displays some of his collection of 1947 to 1955 Lionel locomotives and cars on the shelves behind his 12x20-foot layout.

The Lionel Santa Fe set with the F3A-B-A diesel pair and the Scale Operating Boxcar from page 20 of the 1953 Lionel catalog.

His 12x20-foot layout is a walk-in U-shape, so he can reach all of the tracks from the center operating area. The layout is essentially two ovals wrapped dog bone–style around the tabletop. A third oval runs around the mountain. There are several passing sidings and crossovers, so trains can roam over the entire layout.

The automobiles and trucks are all from the same 1950s era. The majority of the buildings are Plasticville, but all of the accessories and, of course, all of the locomotives and cars are Lionel—and all from that early 1950s era.

Both of the Lionel F3A-B-A diesels from the 1952 catalog, with Lionel's iconic orange Baby Ruth box and white Operating Milk Car in the background.

TWO SMALL LAYOUTS

From 1937 to 1946 in *Model Builder* magazine, and in Lionel's books, Lionel provided dozens of layout plans that were also accompanied by an isometric drawing of how realistic that plan would be with hills, rivers, tunnels, buildings, and, of course, trains and a spattering of Lionel's accessories.

These plans went several steps beyond a simple oval in providing enough track and the proper wiring for two trains to operate. These plans, known as Two O Gauge Layout Ideas, were first published in the October 1939 issue *Model Builder*.

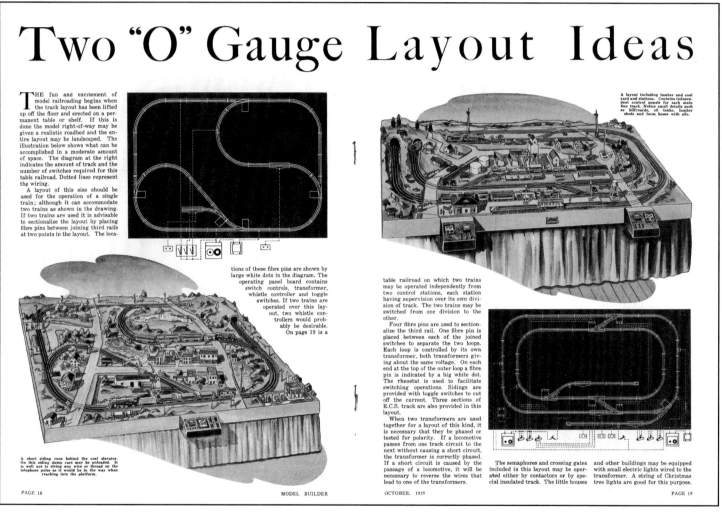

This compact layout at left fills a 6x10-foot area, an awkward size to cover with 4x8-foot sheets of plywood, but in the 1930s and 1940s, 1x4 or 1x6 boards were far more common. The round-roof dormer of the station identifies it as the stamped-steel No. 136 Illuminated Station that Lionel produced prior to World War II. The building at the lower right is Lionel's No. 436 Power Station to house a second transformer. One of the No. 156 Illuminated Station Platforms is used on the far left to suggest a town, and there's a No. 97 Electric Coal Elevator with two tracks spaced to allow coal be dumped on the far side and loaded on the near side. The layout is wired with three electrically isolated blocks, but only one train can be operated at a time—the second train can be parked on the far upper left or where the passenger train is stopped. This is the simple way to assemble a Lionel layout for two trains: use two ovals. The two crossovers allow either train to move from one oval to the other as described in *The Lionel Train Book* and in *The Big Book of Lionel*.

TWO LARGE LAYOUTS

The artist who created the Attic Railroad that appeared in the November 1941 *Model Builder* magazine managed to make the illustration appear at least twice as large as the track plan below it. Lionel's artists preformed similar feats in the catalogs, making the trains look longer, more closely coupled, and lower than they were. The letter As are track sections that must be cut to fit, and the 1/2 OS markings are half straights. All the other sections are O-31 curves and standard straights and O-31 switches. There is no wiring diagram with this plan, but there are three trains. If the sidings were insulated with fiber pins in the third rails and connected with on-off switches, two trains could be parked, the passenger train in the lower left, and the Union Pacific *M10000* streamliner in the upper center, while the third train (also a passenger train!) could run around the mainline.

In the 1930s and 1940s, Lionel brought the dream of a vast railraod network into two-dimensional reality with the illustrations of track plans in *Model Builder* magazine, the *Handbook for Model Builders*, and company catalogs. The illustrations were always stylized to portray the trains with the proportions of the real ones, rather than the somewhat stubby appearance of most of Lionel's toy locomotives and cars. The area of the layout also was exaggerated, a bit like it might appear if photographed with a wide-angle lens. As a result, a ping-pong-table-size model railroad looked almost as spacious as a tennis court.

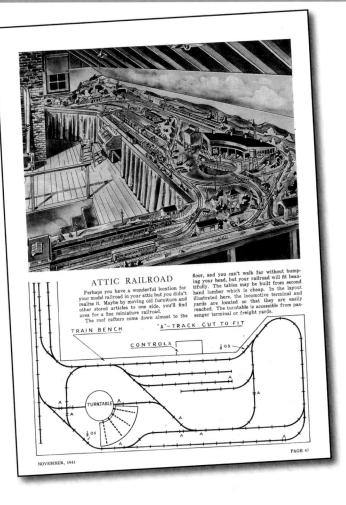

This Drawing Board Layout was published in the March 1944 issue of *Model Builder* magazine as a dream layout. The track plan's proportions do not match that of the isometric drawing, even though the track arrangement is the same. The plan would require something in the order of 30x40 feet. The isometric is much more compressed, however, and with 31-inch minimum diameter curves, it could probably be assembled in as little as 20x20 feet. The plan has a few really interesting areas including the sweeping S curve at the far right (which should be done with 72-inch curves), the six 45-degree crossings on the tracks leading to the roundhouse and turntable, and the complex of alternate routes in the upper right. There's a No. 115 Illuminated Station in the lower left, a string of three No. 155 Illuminated Freight Sheds just below the six 45-degree crossings, and two of Lionel's pre–Word War II No. 440N Light-Position Signal Bridges on the far right and far left center. The layout is essentially an inner and an outer oval with several choices of cut-off routes for reversing trains. You're on your own for a piece-by-piece plan and wiring, however.

PART V

SIXTIES SURVIVAL WITH GENERAL MILLS

LIONEL'S PLASTIC RICO STATION

Mike Sadowski assembled the Rico Station kit as Lionel intended.

The Fundimensions division of General Mills that produced the Lionel products from 1969 to 1985 was driven by the Craftmaster paint-by-numbers success and the MPC line of plastic automobile and aircraft kits. No hobby dealer was really surprised then when Lionel began to offer plastic kits to build railroad buildings and industries.

Ironically, the best-selling Lionel railroad station in history was probably the kit to build a plastic replica of the Rico, Colorado, station, first produced in 1976. The irony was that the real station was on the narrow gauge portion of the Rio Grande Southern Railroad, and Lionel never offered the trains that stopped at that station. However, the station was a classic, originally tooled in HO scale by Heljan in Denmark and later reproduced in both N scale (tiny 1/160 scale) and O scale.

So why Rico? Most likely because the design already existed for the HO model, so the tooling would be less expensive. The station itself was a beautiful Victorian with gingerbread in the eaves and a cupola. It looked more like something found in New Jersey than Colorado.

While the model was too large for most layouts, clever modelers took a razor saw to the parts and cut the freight station from the passenger station to obtain two buildings for the price of one. Over the years, Lionel also offered the model in several colors. In 1990, Lionel offered the station as a stamped-aluminum assembled structure.

Larry LaJambe painted his shortened Rico Station in ornate turn-of-the-century style, then weathered it.

Michael Ulewicz used two Lionel Rico Station (No. 6-62709) kits to create this long depot. He cut the freight station from one of the kits, turned it front to back, and installed it on the opposite end of the station.

LIONEL'S PLASTIC BUILDING KITS

Lionel called this kit the 836K Coaling Station, but it was actually a reasonable replica of a mine tipple. Here, it is being used with Lionel ore cars on the Lionel Visitor's Center layout.

Under the Fundimensions umbrella, Lionel products were marketed as inexpensive toys. By looking at Lionel's 75th anniversary catalog, it wouldn't take long to realize these were not the massive trains your grandfather coveted. The 1975 Lionel catalog does not even include the larger O Gauge track; only the inexpensive O-27 track with brown metal ties is listed.

That catalog only included five small O-27 steam locomotives: two versions of a 2-4-0, a 2-4-2, the smallest 4-4-2 Lionel had yet offered, and a tiny 4-6-4 Hudson. The diesels are all the toylike O-27 models with small bodies and large trucks, including an Alco FA-1 and FB-1, a small NW2 switcher, a small F3A, GP7, GP20, and U36B, and a compact version of the Pennsylvania Railroad's double-ended electric. The only bright spots in the offerings were the freight cars. These included the single-door boxcar, plug-door reefer, Pennsylvania-style four-bay covered hopper, stock car, and triple-deck automobile car that have survived for more than 30 years to become staples of Lionel's Traditional line.

Fundimensions was, however, utilizing what it knew best, using injection-molded plastic to begin a series of buildings for Lionel fans of the 1950s and 1960s. The first of the Lionel plastic kits was a single-stall brick engine house introduced in 1974. For 1975, Lionel had a small passenger station (that Lionel labeled a No. 6-28 787 Freight Station), a small water tower with a brick base, and No. 2783 Freight Station kit (which was later retooled as the Smoking Hobo Shack with six pewter hobos and a smoke unit).

A number of other kits appeared through the late 1970s, including the barrel platform, signal tower, and the largest of the Lionel plastic kits, the 16-inch-tall grain elevator. Most of these well-detailed kits were rereleased in the early 1990s. If Fundimensions left a Lionel legacy, it included two things: It helped bring Lionel back from the dead, and it produced the tooling for these plastic kits that appear on thousands of Lionel layouts today.

This massive grain elevator was offered by Lionel as one of a series of plastic building kits in 1976.

A Lionel Pumping Station operates across the tracks from the oil company's supply shed on Larry LaJambe's layout. Larry repainted and weathered the Lionel plastic Freight Platform kit.

BARGAIN ACTION

The engineers and designers at Fundimensions created a number of plastic accessories that could provide the action that dads and granddads had come to expect from Lionel. Unfortunately, the catalogs in the late 1970s did not include a single motorized accessory—no log loaders or coal elevators or magnetic cranes or operating milk cars—nothing.

The one page of the 1975 catalog labeled "Operating Accessories" included an electrically triggered crossing gate, a banjo signal, target signs, a two-light highway flasher, and a combination crossing gate/flasher. Oh, yes, the Automatic Gateman was there, too. There was also a mechanically operated crossing gate and mechanically operated semaphore signals—both were actuated by the weight of the train pressing down on a lever between the ties.

Lionel did devise some clever manually operated accessories, all inexpensive enough to be included in the low-cost train sets. The manually operated No. 2712 Log Loading Mill and manually operated No. 2722 Barrel Loader were both introduced in 1979. Eventually, Fundimensions did realize that there was a much larger and more profitable market for higher-priced trains, and the line was gradually improved during the late 1970s and early 1980s.

Lionel purchased American Flyer trains and tooling in 1972, but did not release the first American Flyer reproduction, the No. 2300 Automatic Oil Drum Loader (where a

Lionel introduced more inexpensive plastic kits in the 1990s, including this Operating Log Loader.

forklift truck pushes barrels onto a ramp and the barrels are dumped into a waiting gondola), until 1983. The Operating Control Tower (where one workman moves out of the second-floor door while the other climbs the stairs) was also reintroduced in 1983 to begin, at last, the reincarnation of the Lionel legacy.

Lionel offered this very simple plastic kit to build a manually operated Barrel Loader (No.6-12706) like the one in front of the 464R Operating Sawmill on Michael Ulewicz's layout.

A Lionel Freight Platform (No. 6-12773) and the Operating Switch Tower on Michael Ulewicz's layout. The Operating Switch Tower has been offered in several colors, even one with simulated flames. The tower man moves out onto the platform when the operating button is pushed.

Lionel offered the American Flyer Oil Drum Loader under its own label. It has a small forklift that shoves the barrels off the platform into (hopefully) an awaiting boxcar with an open door.

LIONEL HO SCALE

Lionel's box art for its HO scale sets from 1959.

Lionel just could not ignore the phenomenal growth of HO scale in the 1950s, so finally, in 1959, Lionel took the plunge. Many of its HO scale products were direct copies of Athearn's models, and the company apparently repackaged some Athearn models, as well.

By 1966, when Lionel bailed out of the HO market, the Lionel line included examples of a variety of steam, diesel, and even electric locomotives, freight cars, and passenger cars.

In 1976, Lionel produced its first HO scale ready-to-run replicas of the Alco FA-2 and FB-2, EMD GP9 and General Electric U18B diesel locomotives, and a replica of the Southern Pacific class GS-4 Northern 4-8-4 in SP orange, yellow, and black and in the red, white, and blue of the American Freedom Train. In 1976, the American Freedom Train was a traveling museum train with displays

of America's history, including copies of the Declaration of Independence and the U.S. Constitution in a seven-car train that toured the country.

Eventually, Lionel realized that it could sell an O Gauge locomotive or car for several times the price on an equivalent HO model, but both required the same advertising and marketing effort. And in the 1950s and 1960s, Lionel had little competition in its market segment, so producing HO scale products was temporarily abandoned.

Lionel dabbled in HO again in 1985. The structures only lasted about a year in the Lionel line.

Lionel tried HO scale again in 2003 with excellent scale models of the Union Pacific Gas Turbine (see pages 228 and 229) and the Union Pacific 4-6-6-4 Challenger, yet the sales did not meet company expectations.

Lionel offered 72-foot passenger cars in 1959 that were virtual duplicates of Athearn's models.

Lionel's No. 0050 self-powered Gang Car and its replica of Athearn's *Little Hustler* were produced from 1959 to 1966.

Lionel was back again in the small-scale market with a 12-page catalog for 1976 that included a well-detailed Southern Pacific GS-4 and a range of three modern diesels.

THE ICE BUSINESS

The workman on the Lionel Ice Depot automatically pushes blocks of clear plastic "ice" into the open rooftop hatch of one of the Lionel Ice Cars on Michael Ulewicz's layout.

The Lionel Ice Depots, produced from 1955 to 1957 and reintroduced in 1982, were activated by a solenoid with a plunger to operate the lever that moves the workman who pushes the ice into waiting Ice Cars.

The Lionel No. 352 Operating Ice Depot was first produced in 1955 and was one of the first operating accessories to reappear during the General Mills period in 1982. The depot includes a conveyor where clear plastic blocks of "ice" are unloaded at the bottom and then transported up to the elevated house. When the operating button is depressed, a metal lever opens the hatch on the roof of the special "ice car," while a workman shoves a block of ice off the end of the platform and into the car.

Lionel has offered the accessory in a variety of colors, including a recent version that uses brown plastic cubes to simulate cardboard boxes and a United Parcel Service boxcar with that special roof hatch.

There was no Lionel "ice car" that would unload the cubes of ice, so some Lionel railroaders used one of the Operating Boxcars to unload the ice into a small box. Except for the Operating Cattle Car and Log and Coal Dump Cars, Lionel has seldom produced a single car that could both be loaded and unloaded by remote control. However, the company has offered accessories to load cars, such as the Ice Depot and other cars, such as the Operating Milk Car, to unload products.

LIONEL'S ROADSIDE DINERS

Since the company's earliest days, Lionel has offered a variety of buildings—from the 1920s-era series of houses complete with front and backyards to the recent Lionelville series of ready-built stores, playgrounds, and even a carnival (pages 226 and 227). There also have been at least three different roadside diners.

The iconic American diner got its name because it looked like a railroad car, and many of them were. In fact, most were converted trolley cars. To re-create one, Lionel could use existing passenger car tooling, making a diner a natural choice for a new product. Lionel's first was the stamped-steel No. 442 Landscaped Diner, introduced in 1938.

In 1988, Lionel mounted one of its O-27-size Pullman cars on a base and fitted it with a smoke unit to become the Roadside Diner with Smoke. It has been reintroduced in a variety of colors. In 2006, Lionel offered the No. 12952 Big L Diner as a plastic kit.

Lionel's latest diner is not based on a railroad passenger car. Known as Irene's Diner, it is an all-new replica of the stainless-steel-covered modern era restaurant and has a full interior with lights.

The No. 12722 Operating Roadside Diner, with smoke, from 1988 on Gino Szymanowski's layout.

The Lionel No. 12952 Diner was sold as a plastic kit. It is situated near the Lionel No. 32998 Hobby Shop (see page 224) on Mike Sadowski's layout.

PART VI

THE REAWAKENING WITH RICHARD KUGHN

LIONMASTER LOCOMOTIVES

The postwar-era No. 2046 Lionel O Scale New York Central Hudson is, perhaps, the most famous of Lionel's steam locomotives, but the newer (and slightly smaller) LionMaster model has far more detail and performance. The new Hudson also has TrainMaster Command Control.

Lionel enthusiast Richard Kughn took over the position of chairman and CEO of Lionel in 1985. His driving force is generally credited with bringing Lionel back to life after its General Mills ownership, but, in truth, Lionel had already started to become the company it is today. Richard Kughn and his crew just made certain that would happen.

At the time, Lionel's customers were demanding ever higher levels of detail on their trains at lower prices. So in the 1990s, Lionel shifted the production of its more common items, like track and operating accessories, to China. Most of the new operating accessories and the larger locomotives were also produced in China.

In the 1997 catalog, Lionel identified the models that were made in America with small American flags, a step that seemed more to highlight what was not made in America than what was. The gradual shift to producing the entire Lionel line in China made it possible for Lionel to offer products at prices that the market would pay, without totally loosing the "Made in America" image.

Lionel customers also demanded large locomotives like the Union Pacific 4-8-8-4 articulated Big Boy. However,

in accurate 1/48 scale, the model locomotive would not negotiate even a 72-inch curve, much less a 32- or 36-inch curve. Lionel solved the problem by creating a new series of large steam locomotives to operate on curves as small as 31 inches.

In 2000, Lionel gave its fans the first of the LionMaster series—a replica of the Union Pacific 4-6-6-4 Challenger, a slightly smaller version of the Big Boy. The LionMaster model could negotiate 31-inch curves and was a near-scale 28 inches long. In 2001, Lionel offered an exact-scale Union Pacific 4-6-6-4 Challenger. It was 32 inches long and would operate only on 72-inch or larger curves.

Lionel refers to its "exact-scale" models as Standard O. The company's slightly smaller models—including the LionMaster line—are called Traditional, and the least-expensive and smallest locomotives and cars are now called O Gauge, but were once referred to as O-27. The exact scale varies, with Standard O being close to exact 1/48 scale, the Traditional being somewhat smaller (in the range of 1/50 to 1/55 scale), and O Gauge or O-27 models in the range of 1/50 to as small as 1/64 scale.

The No. 2770 Standard O replica of the New York Central 4-8-2 Mohawk, produced in 2006, was 25 inches long.

Lionel's No. 226E was the top-of-the-line of O Gauge locomotive in 1938. It was a shortened version of the Scale Hudson but with two, rather than four, leading wheels.

The No. 5418 Lionel Hudson was one of the more recent production models built to 1/48 scale, but it lacks some of the details of 1940 model.

Lionel introduced the LionMaster label to apply to massive, but semi-scale locomotives. Lionel has done this before. In 1938, its second die-cast steam locomotive, the 226E, was a smaller-size replica of the exact 1/48 scale Hudson of 1937. The 226E looked very much like the larger-scale model (although it lacked two of the four lead wheels—it was a 2-6-4, the Hudson a 4-6-4), and it was one of the best-performing models Lionel made. It also was about a fourth the price of the scale Hudson.

The LionMaster locomotives are significantly smaller than true O scale—in fact, nearly all of Lionel's locomotives are smaller than true O scale. However, many of them have their proportions altered in the process of shrinking to underscale size. The LionMaster models effectively retain their accurate shapes and portions.

The LionMaster series includes replicas of the massive 6,000-horsepower, 12-wheeled diesels like the Electro-Motive Division (EMD) SD80MAC, SD90MAC, and the other modern monster, the General Electric Dash 9-44W. In comparison, the O Gauge replica of the EMD SD80MAC is 19½ inches long, while the LionMaster SD80MAC is 17½ inches long.

The LionMaster series also includes steam locomotives like the New York Central 4-6-4 Hudson, the Pennsylvania Railroad class T-1 4-4-4-4 Duplex steam locomotive, the Southern Pacific 4-8-8-2 Cab Forward, and the Union Pacific 4-8-8-4 Big Boy steam locomotive. The Lionel Standard O scale model of the Union Pacific 4-8-8-4 Big Boy was offered in 1999, but it would only operate on 72-inch curves and was 32 inches long. In contrast, the 22-inch-long LionMaster version of the Big Boy will operate on smaller radius curves, including the O-31 curves.

The LionMaster replica of the Norfolk & Western 2-6-6-4 Class A articulated.

Lionel's Standard O 2007 exact-scale replica of the EMD E7A and E7B with operating diaphragms between the two locomotives.

THE HUDSON LEGENDS

The New York Central class J3a Hudson 4-6-4 has become the image of Lionel steam locomotives. It has been featured on several Lionel catalog covers—from its introduction in 1937 as the Lionel 700E to the 100th anniversary catalog in 2000. The Lionel 700E was exact 1/48 scale, a near perfect replica that was 24½ inches long.

In the intervening 70 years, Lionel produced a truly bewildering array of 4-6-4 locomotives, each bearing "New York Central" across the tender. They ranged in size from being as small as 19 inches long to as large as the 700E. Clearly, the exact-scale Hudson was expensive to make, so Lionel made it less complex and cheaper every year, shrinking the replica slightly, to 24 inches in 1950.

This full-size steam locomotive, like most others, had a unique combination of domes across the top of the boiler, a distinctive cab and boiler front, and other details peculiar to this specific railroad and class of locomotives. Lionel offered at least a half-dozen different superstructures like this as New York Central locomotives, none with domes or a cab remotely like the J3a. Some, like the No. 5412 from 2000, were similar to the J3a, but had different domes on the top of the boiler. In truth, the New York Central did have other classes of Hudsons, but Lionel's model matched none of them.

Lionel boldly reintroduced the exact-scale New York Central J3a Hudson in 1984 with the number 783 on the cab (the original No. 700E carried the number 5344). In 2000, Lionel offered a reproduction of that model plated in real gold with number 1900 on the cab. Lionel also offered a black version with the number 5344 and later had one with the number 5340 on the sides of the cab.

The LionMaster semi-scale Hudsons (NYC No. 5422 and Boston & Albany versions were available), introduced in 2003, retained the proportions of the true O scale models, but were just 22 inches long.

Lionel's legendary Scale Hudson, as it was in 1990.

Lionel's latest reincarnation of the Scale New York Central Hudson from 1990, in operation on Michael Raschig's layout, has all the details of the original 1937 version.

TRUE SCALE LIONEL LOCOMOTIVES

In the late 1930s and early 1940s, several model railroad enthusiasts built exact-scale layouts in their homes or at model railroad clubs. Many of these O scale model railroaders used Lionel's replicas of the New York Central 4-6-4 Hudson and Pennsylvania Railroad class B-6 0-6-0 switching locomotive on their exact-scale railroads. Lionel offered both locomotives with drivers and wheels with smaller flanges and conversion kits to change the power from three-rail AC current to two-rail DC current. Or the modeler could retain the three-rail system and hand-make track with an outside third rail.

Flash forward to the late 1990s, and Lionel was again producing accurate O scale locomotive and cars. These had the traditional Lionel oversize wheel flanges and monster-size couplers. Again, modelers adapted the Lionel locomotives and cars to operate on scale-size rail. Those who were willing to accept the center third rail had a third option: Operate the Lionel models as-is, but use more realistic track and avoid any of the undersize models, even the LionMaster locomotives. Because these model railroads were scale in all but the track, they became know as hi-rail model railroads. (Not to be confused with the real railroad's maintenance trucks with both standard rubber tires and additional sets of flanged wheels—vehicles are known as hi-railers.)

Most of the hi-rail modelers removed the Lionel couplers and substituted correct-scale couplers—either nonoperating one-piece dummy couplers or operating couplers produced by Kadee. Most modelers also replaced the wheels with ones that had slightly smaller flanges. Most hi-railers used Gargraves track, which has somewhat smaller rails but more accurate wood ties and a blackened center rail. More recently, some hi-rail modelers are using the Lionel FasTrack with the ties and ballast weathered with stains.

Lionel's Hudson and 0-6-0 were the company's first scale locomotives, and both were reproduced in the late 1990s. Lionel offered the Pennsylvania Railroad class T-1 4-4-4-4 as

an exact-scale model in 2000. Lionel's model was 31½ inches long. There were two versions: the three-rail, designed for Lionel's track with a minimum curve size of 72 inches, and the two-rail model, which has smaller flanges and was designed to operate on two-rail "scale" track.

Lionel produced a number of articulated exact-scale steam locomotives, including a 2001 scale replica of the Union Pacific 4-6-6-4 Challenger that was 32 inches long.

Lionel also offered the 2-8-0 Harriman Consolidation in 2001 as an exact-scale model, except, of course, for the oversize wheel flanges and the coupler on the tender. It was small enough, however, to operate on 31-inch curves. The Lionel replica of the Pennsylvania Railroad 4-4-2, the Pennsylvania Railroad B-6 0-6-0, and the Shay from 1992 were other exact-scale locomotives that could operate on 31-inch curves.

Lionel is using the Standard O series to produce models that were only seen on some of the lesser-known real railroads across the country. The Standard O locomotives are more expensive than Lionel's Traditional O series, so fewer are produced, which makes it economically feasible to select locomotives that were only used by one or two railroads.

Recently, Lionel has brought out a number of locomotives that were unique to the Chesapeake & Ohio, including the 2-6-6-2 and the renowned C&O 2-6-6-6 Allegheny. Lionel already had a Standard O replica of the USRA Pacific 4-6-2, but it also produced the somewhat different C&O 4-6-2 with a completely different body and tender to match the full-size locomotive more precisely.

Lionel continues to expand its choices of exact O scale freight cars with models of modern-era cars like Airslide two-bay covered hoppers to simulated wood stock cars, reefers, boxcars, and a caboose as shown on pages 194 and 195. Lionel also has a range of passenger cars with exact O scale width and height, but slightly shorter lengths as shown on pages 192 and 193.

The Santa Fe 2-8-8-2 articulated is another precise replica of a real steam locomotive in exact 1/48 scale.

Lionel's 4-6-6-4 Challenger is a full-scale model, but it also will negotiate 31-inch curves.

The Pennsylvania Railroad 4-8-2 Mountain is one of Lionel's massive locomotives; with a wheelbase so long, it will only negotiate 54-inch or larger curves.

The three-truck Western Maryland Shay geared locomotive has been offered by Lionel in several road names.

LIONEL CLASSICS

Lionel's replica of its 1937 Union Pacific *M10000* on the Milwaukee Model Railroad Club layout.

One of the legacies that Richard Kughn established at Lionel was the idea to reproduce the most spectacular stamped-steel toys from the company's history. So in 1988, Lionel introduced the first of an ongoing series of these stamped-steel toys as part of the Lionel Classics series.

At the time, the original Lionel toys were becoming extremely expensive to buy, so a number of Lionel fans wanted replicas, either to display or to run, so they wouldn't have to fear damaging an irreplaceable heirloom.

As part of Kuhn's plan, the Lionel Classics are extremely faithful replicas. They are so exact, in fact, that each is labeled clearly with letters LTI and a copyright date, so as not to be confused with originals. These replicas are actually better in every way than the originals because modern production methods allow

In 1989, Lionel reproduced its own 1930s-era stamped-steel tinplate locomotives and cars, including this replica of the 22½-inch-long No. 1384E Standard Gauge 2-4-0.

much better tolerances and modern casting methods are more reliable. New dies were made for the reproductions, using the originals and computer scanning with CAD (computer-assisted design) to re-create the exact shape of the original. The earliest Lionel trains were dipped in paint because spray painting had not yet been perfected. These newer models are, of course, spray-painted with a perfect finish.

In the Lionel Classics, every detail of the original is re-created, usually including the motor design, gearing, trucks, and couplers. The models carry the same nameplates and lettering with only that LTI stamping (and a better-than-original finish) to distinguish them from the originals.

As part of the series, Lionel has produced replicas of both Standard Gauge locomotives and cars and the O Gauge locomotives and cars, as well as some of the more spectacular accessories like the Hell Gate Bridge. Each year, Lionel introduces more of the company's stamped-steel history. Lionel also has reproduced its 1912 slot car set and its windup (clockwork) power boats from the 1930s.

The first Standard Gauge locomotive Lionel reproduced in 1988 was a replica of the 1390E, a black 2-4-2 with domes in brass and the piping in bare copper and with red-spoked pilot wheels and trailing wheels and drivers. A replica of the 1384E 2-4-0 steam locomotive in a gray-and-red finish was added to the series of Lionel reproductions in 1989. Reproductions of the Standard Gauge searchlight car, stock car, and caboose were offered at the same time.

Lionel has also offered reproductions of some of the stamped-steel O Gauge trains from 1930s, including the Union Pacific *M10000* articulated passenger train (see pages 78 and 79).

TAKE A RIDE INSIDE

Imagine riding inside your Lionel train as it rumbles its way around your layout. That was finally possible when Lionel introduced its Railscope in-cab video camera and monitor in 1988. Railscope's video was black and white, but the locomotive to send the signal and the monitor to receive and view the videos was included. All you had to do was put the Railscope locomotive on the track, connect the wires to Railscope, and "climb inside the cab" of your Lionel engine for a trip.

Railscope functioned very well. The camera lens was set to be in focus from four inches to infinity with a 22-degree wide angle so that you could see far beyond the ends of the ties. Lionel offered Railscope in a pair of HO FA-2 diesels, in an O Gauge EMD GP7, and in a Large Scale 0-4-0. No matter what scale your track was, you could enjoy a Railscope.

Lionel offered Railscope with O Gauge, Large Scale, and HO scale locomotives (pictured here).

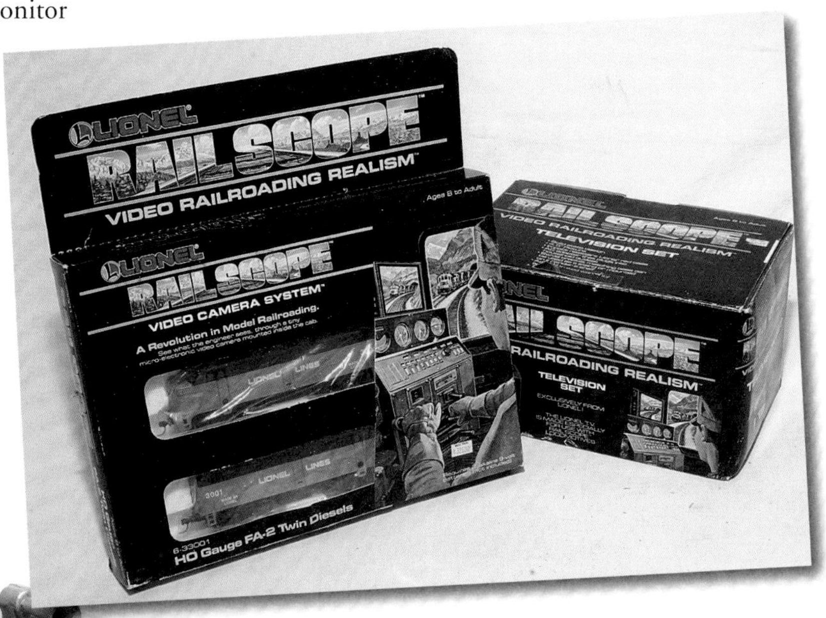

The nose of Lionel's FA2 HO scale diesel was cut out to accommodate the video camera's lens.

Lionel supplied its own monitor for Railscope.

Lionel even created a contest in 1989 for the best video produced with Railscope. Chuck Sartor, from Mizell Trains in Westminster, Colorado, won it.

For most of us Lionel fans, the trip around the layout was extremely disappointing. The joy of operating Lionel trains is usually about 80 percent imagination and 20 percent reality. We imagine our train pulling out of the yard, past the signal tower and the urban apartments and industries, to rumble through cornfields, over the rivers, through tunnels, and up and around the mountain passes. Railscope brought home the cold, hard reality that most of that world existed only in our imagination.

If you had a Lionel layout on the living room floor, you saw a collection of closeups of table legs, couch legs, electrical outlets, baseboards, and just plain floor or carpet. Even if your layout was covered with scenery, the tracks ran down the edges of the table so, at best, only half of the view was of scenery. The rest was a jarring look at your train room in wide-angle vision and in black and white at that. Railscope was a product created from the designers' imaginations, but the reality of in-cab black-and-white travel was not what they had imagined at all.

MODERN PASSENGER CARS

Passenger trains are part of the romance of railroading, part of the reason Lionel has offered them since its earliest days. However, Lionel always faced a problem when designing exact-scale passenger cars: They are about twice the length of a freight car and that can cause problems on the tight curves of Lionel track.

Lionel's largest curved track sections produce a circle that is 72 inches in diameter, but the curved tracks in most Lionel sets are just 31-inch diameter circles. With such tight curves, Lionel was forced to make toylike cars and locomotives because there had to be enough clearance beneath the car or locomotive for both trucks (and the coupler that is mounted on each of the trucks) to swivel out (sometimes way out) from beneath the body when the locomotive or car is moving through a curve. With exact-scale length passenger cars, the overhang is just too much for anything but a 54-inch or larger circle. In fact, some of the larger locomotives in the Standard O series will only operate on 72-inch or larger curves.

So in 1952, Lionel elected to produce passenger cars with exact-scale width and height but to shorten them about 20 percent to create a 15-inch-long car. More

than 50 years later, in 2005, Lionel created a new series of scale width and height cars that were 19 inches long, only about 10 percent shorter than exact scale—a practice followed even by HO train makers like Athearn. This resulted in a car that was a scale 72 feet long rather than the correct scale 86-foot length.

The best compromise between the cars looking too pudgy and being too long for most curves seems to be about 72 scale feet. By that measure, the newest Standard O scale passenger should be about 21 inches long, but they are just 19 inches, including almost two inches for extended couplers on each end (making the model about 72 scale feet long overall).

Nearly all of Lionel's Standard O passenger cars, including its replicas of the heavyweight steel cars, its series of extruded aluminum smooth-side and corrugated-side cars, and even the replicas of the modern double-deck Amtrak cars are about 72 scale feet long. Recently, Lionel has produced very limited series of scale-length corrugated-side aluminum extrusion cars that are 21 inches long, virtually exact scale in length, as well as in width and height.

Lionel introduced the first 15-inch-long extruded-aluminum corrugated streamline cars in 1952.

When Lionel shifted production to China, it was able include super details like complete interiors with a half-dozen passengers at the prices of the less-detailed cars.

Lionel produced a second series of 15-inch-long extruded-aluminum corrugated cars in 2003 and offered some painted for roads like the New York Central.

SCALE FREIGHT CARS

Lionel introduced exact-scale freight cars in 1940, but before the decade ended, they were dropped from the line for nearly 40 years. It wasn't until the late 1980s that Lionel once again began to offer the option of exact-scale locomotives, freight cars, and passenger cars.

Most of today's Lionel exact-scale freight cars are in the Standard O category. Most of the cars include both Lionel's current knuckle couplers mounted on the trucks and a second set of couplers that you can install yourself on the carbody (after removing the Lionel couplers).

Lionel introduces a car or more each year, so any full listing here would soon be out of date. However, I knew Lionel had offered the exact-scale hi-railer hobbyists a host of freight cars, so I looked back through catalogs to see just how many. I've listed them in groups by era, and, as you see, there are representative examples of just about any type of freight car you would want from both the steam era and the modern era. And, if you choose, all will operate on Lionel track.

Here they are:

Compare Lionel's 2006 exact-scale stock car with its O Gauge version. The exact-scale car is about 20 percent larger.

Steam (and First-Generation Diesel) Era
- 40-foot USRA single-sheathed wood boxcars
- 40-foot single-door steel boxcars
- 50-foot double-door boxcars
- 50-foot double-door boxcars with operating end doors for loading automobiles
- A New York Central wood caboose (the remake of Lionel's 1940 car)
- The steel bay-window caboose and 1940s-era Baltimore & Ohio prototype rib side caboose
- The extended vision cupola caboose
- The Union Pacific steel cupola caboose
- The Reading Railroad–style four-window cupola caboose
- The Pennsylvania Railroad two-window style class N5 centered cupola caboose
- The Pennsylvania railroad porthole window class N5C caboose
- The Pere Marquette two-window center cupola caboose
- The 50-foot cylindrical covered hoppers with four bays
- PS-4 50-foot flatcars
- PS-5 50-foot gondolas
- PS-5 covered gondolas
- The 50-foot "piggyback" TOFC (trailer on flat cars)

- Wood-side and all-metal ice bunker 40-foot reefers
- 40-foot plug-door ice bunker reefers
- 40-foot stock cars
- 40-foot wood milk TANK cars
- 8,000-gallon tank cars
- Steel mill slag and hot metal cars with glowing loads of simulated molten slag
- Steel mill hot metal cars with rotating hot metal drums

Modern Era
- 50-foot x-post sliding door "Railbox" boxcars
- 60-foot x-post Pullman Standard single-door boxcars
- 60-foot x-post Pullman Standard double-door boxcars
- PS-2 two-bay covered hoppers
- PS2CD three-bay covered hoppers
- ACF Centerflow two-bay and three-bay covered hoppers
- Two-bay offset-side hoppers
- Three-bay 40-foot rib-side hoppers
- Bathtub coal gondolas
- Intermodal well and articulated cars
- 50-foot plug door mechanical reefers
- Unibody modern tank cars
- Tank Train tank cars

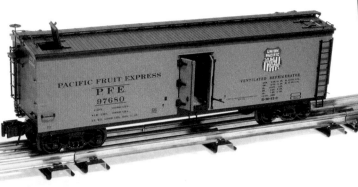

Lionel's replica of the Pacific Fruit Express wood refrigerator car has opening doors and roof hatches with compartments inside each for the cardboard blocks of "ice"—all exact replicas of the full-size car.

Lionel's 1950s-era exact-scale stock cars were introduced in 2001 with full underbody detail and exact scale width and length.

Lionel's scale tank train car and an intermodal well car with containers on the Lionel Visitor's Center layout.

MEN AT WORK

The box- or barrel-unloading boxcar was an early Lionel action car.

O ver the decades, Lionel devised some incredible methods to make it appear that workmen really were working to load or unload its freight cars. The first of its Operating Boxcars cars to feature an operating workman was introduced in 1947, as was the Operating Milk Car (see pages 130 and 131) where a workman moved slowly to push the milk containers out the door. In 1949, Lionel added an operating boxcar where a workman slowly pushed boxes out the door.

The workman's mechanism was similar to that in the Lionel Milk Car, but much simpler because the workman was actuated by a magnetic disc suspended beneath the car. The disc was pulled down by the magnetic attraction of Lionel's electromagnetic operating track. The milk cans had magnets and needed to remain upright, while the boxes or mail bags could just lie there and be pushed randomly onto the platform. The basic shove-it-out-the door series included boxcars, as well as poultry cars and mail cars.

Lionel has also offered a variety of accessories where the workmen applied signs to a billboard or labored mightily to repair the track or to scrap a diesel.

The workman in the No. 9301 U.S. Mail Operating Boxcar pushed the mail bags out the door. If the No. 12729 Operating Mail Pickup was positioned correctly, it would grab the mail bag as the train passed by. The real railroads used very similar equipment but with Railway Post Office passenger cars, not boxcars.

The workman on the Operating Billboard Sign moves his roller up and down the face of the billboard to push the paper onto the sign.

Welcome to Lionelville

The Lionel No. 34144 Scrap Yard has animated workers with the flash of a cutting torch dissembling the F3A cab next to a No. 24105 Track Gang busily setting a new rail—both are on FasTrack on the Chicagoland Lionel Railroad Club layout.

MODERN INTERMODAL

The Southern Pacific Intermodal Crane on the Lionel Visitor's Center layout moves forward and back, and the container rack grips and lifts the containers and moves them right to left.

The real railroads began offering piggyback service, shipping complete highway trailers on flatcars (called TOFC service) in the early 1950s. By 1959, Lionel had its own replica of a piggyback flatcar with two trailers. Later, Lionel offered flatcars with single 35-foot trailer loads. When Lionel's exact-scale replica of the PS-4 50-foot flatcar was produced in 2006, it was soon available with a pair of replica 24-foot trailers.

In the late 1950s, the real railroads began to use longer and longer cars—from 79 feet up to 86 feet—and Lionel decided against re-creating those longer cars because scale models would not work on Lionel's tight curves. In the 1980s and 1990s, however, the real railroads also began to haul containers as well as highway trailers. The containers could travel on oceangoing ships as well as on highway trailer chassis and on railroad flatcars. This service became known as intermodal transit.

The railroads soon began to order special intermodal cars that would carry a single container or trailer and, later,

a stack of two 40-foot containers. In 2006, Lionel introduced its replicas of the All Purpose Husky-Stack single-unit cars with two stacked 48-foot containers. And Lionel offered replicas of the two-unit articulated TTUX (two-unit articulated intermodal cars with a single 40-foot trailer on each unit) in 1991. In 1993, Lionel introduced the replicas of the Maxi Stack cars with containers stacked two high.

Lionel has also offered two motorized accessories for intermodals. The No. 460P Piggyback Platform used a forklift truck to push the short trailers onto the flatcars. The 1989 Union Pacific Mi-Jack Intermodal Crane rolled on small rubber tires, which were motorized so that the crane could move back and forth down the track. Two jaws grip the containers or release them. The jaws are mounted in a rack that can be moved in and out and from right or left. The accessory allows you to re-create virtually every movement of action found on real life intermodal cranes by remote control.

Lionel's Union Pacific Mi-Jack Intermodal Crane on David Seebach's layout.

The Lionel Maxi Stack Cars with Containers and the articulated TTUX two-unit intermodal cars.

Lionel's No. 460P Piggyback Platform moved trailers onto flatcars at the push of the remote-control button.

LIONEL'S TRAIN DISPATCHERS

On a real railroad, the dispatcher is usually a worker who decides which trains get priority in the system. Traditionally, this dispatcher sits in a control tower with a diagram of most of that particular division of the railroad with lights indicating the positions of trains and the signals and the locations of sidings. Then the dispatcher throws the switches to activate the signals alongside the tracks to tell the engineers of each and every train, if they can proceed, or if they must stop or pull into the next passing siding.

Lionel has not, yet, been able simulate the actual operations of the dispatcher's control panel. That, in my opinion, is the future for Lionel's Legacy system but, for now, consider the dispatcher's legacy in Lionel world.

On the real railroad, the dispatcher was usually located in an elevated building near one of the major freight yards, so he and his crew could see the yard out the windows and the rest of line on their schematic control panel. Some real railroad freight yards, however, have a separate operating system that was not controlled by the dispatcher but by a local tower operator. He or she had a similar schematic to that of the dispatcher, but with every track and every switch in the yard diagramed on the panel.

In Lionel's history, the company has produced a dispatcher's tower, as well as two versions of a switch tower. The No. 445 Switch Tower is a replica of an older clapboard-siding two-story structure with a pyramid-shaped roof. Lionel has produced a number of variations of this accessory, but in most the two figures operate simultaneously.

The No. 192 and later No. 2318 are modern versions of the dispatcher's tower, supported by simulated steel legs and with vast windows. Inside, the No. 192 Control Tower has two dispatchers with feathered plastic bases that move around in circles, propelled by a vibrating plate.

In the larger No. 2318 Elevated Dispatching Station, the dispatcher and his crew inside moved back and forth using the vibrator principle (with plastic feathers beneath bases of the workmen that were activated by vibrating metal base). A radio aerial rotated on the roof. Later versions included Lionel's CrewTalk.

Lionel also produced the No. 334 Operating Dispatch Board that is similar to what might appear inside a passenger station where the arrival and departure times of the trains are posted. Lionel's model includes a workman who runs across the platform as the numbers appear to change on the board.

One workman pops out of the upstairs door while the second runs up and down the stairs on Lionel's No. 445 Switch Tower.

The workman on the No. 334 Operating Dispatch appears to change the arrival and departure times of the trains.

The Elevated Dispatching Station includes a rather crude paper workman who moves around inside—this later version has Lionel's CrewTalk.

The Lionel No. 192 Railroad Control Station from 2000 has workmen inside that move in a never-ending circle.

SPEEDERS AND BURROS

Trains are not the only things that travel down a real railroad's tracks. A variety of inspection and maintenance vehicles are also needed to be sure the track is in perfect condition. Some of these vehicles are simple, small four-wheeled carts propelled by men pumping a teeter-totterlike device, part of the reason they became known as handcars. Today, these vehicles are powered by small gasoline engines and are often called speeders.

There are also a variety of automobiles and trucks that are fitted with special hi-railer devices, which attach small, steel-flanged wheels to each corner to keep the vehicle on the rails, while the rubber tires provide the traction to propel the car or truck.

In addition, the real railroads have small self-propelled cranes, called burro cranes, that are normally used around the locomotive shops to both lift and pull, as well as a number of other track repair and inspection vehicles. Lionel has offered several of these self-propelled little machines.

Lionel has produced a variety of these speeders with full interiors and flashing red roof lights.

The self-powered Rail Bonder appeared in the 2004 catalog. This is a replica of a real railroad car used to join new sections of rail. A pole on the roof could be raised so that the crew can check and measure overhead clearances at bridges and tunnels.

The Lionel No. 18491 replica of the Ballast Tamper was introduced in 2004. When the real railroads replace or clean the crushed rock ballast that retains the wood or concrete ties, these machines pound the crushed rock down so that it will not allow rain to seep in and later freeze.

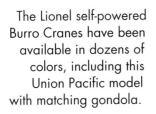

The Lionel self-powered Burro Cranes have been available in dozens of colors, including this Union Pacific model with matching gondola.

Lionel's compact drive mechanism is also used in its four-wheel snowplows.

BRIDGES AND ROAD CROSSINGS

A bridge or a highway crossing is a simple way to suggest scenery on a model railroad layout without actually creating four-foot-high mountains or waist-deep canyons. The majority of Lionel bridges have been designed so that they can be inserted between the track and the table-top or carpet.

The Hell Gate Bridge was Lionel's most massive bridge at 29 inches long, but the Nos. 315 and 317 stamped-steel truss bridges spanned the same gap (24 inches) while looking much, much lighter. Lionel replaced the stamped-steel truss bridge (which Lionel called a trestle bridge) with a 24-inch-span plastic version in 1958. The bridge has been offered with both an arched top and with the top parallel to the bottom. All have stamped-steel bases for strength. Lionel also offered a much more sensational truss bridge in 2002 with the top parallel to the bottom and a 26-inch span. A very toylike plastic 10-inch short extension bridge version of the arched-top truss bridge is also available to simply rest beside the ends of the ties.

Lionel's most popular bridge was its replica of the riveted-steel-plate girder bridge. The cast-metal, rounded-corner

Four Lionel No. 314 Plate Girder Bridges and a single Truss Bridge on the Chicagoland Lionel Railroad Club layout.

Two of the No. 332 Arch Under Bridges on David Seebach's massive layout.

solid-plate, girder-style bridge did not appear until 1940. The cast-metal bridge was replaced by No. 214 Plate Girder Bridge plastic model, with the ends at 45-degree angles, in 1953. Lionel reintroduced the No. 314 cast-metal plate girder bridge in 2002.

One of Lionel's rare bridges that demanded a valley or canyon beneath the tracks is the enduring No. 332 Arch Under Bridge, introduced in stamped steel in 1959 and reintroduced in 1990 in plastic.

As for highway crossings, Lionel was also quick to re-create these, as they were the places where the public most frequently encountered trains. As with the real railroad world where motorists are warned of approaching trains by flashing red lights, crossing gates that block the highway, simple railroad crossing cross bucks, and even workmen waving lanterns, Lionel could have the same devices.

Lionel has offered flashing highway signs and operating highway crossing gates for nearly 100 years. These are the style that Lionel introduced in the 1940s, including the Automatic Gateman.

Until about 10 years ago, however, Lionel's crossing warning devices were all about five times or more larger in scale than the scale of the trains. More recently, however, Lionel has introduced exact-scale replicas of modern highway crossing signs.

Lionel's newer series of correct-size highway crossing signs includes this No. 22934 Mainline Walkout Cantilever Signal. It blinks two pairs of red lights to warn motorists of oncoming trains.

LET THERE BE LIGHT

Right from the start, Lionel locomotives had operating lights, and the interiors of the passenger cars and cabooses glowed. The light added more of the suggestion that there really were living people inside that train. Within a few years, Lionel added the first flashing highway crossing signals and offered the red and green railroad signals that controlled the real trains.

With the room lights dimmed or off, the model railroad glows like a sky full of stars, but each light source implies reality—that there are people inside that station, that the street lights are there for the safety of the pedestrians, and the floodlights do make work easier for workmen. Light, you see, brings life to Lionel.

The Lionel Classic reproduction of the O Gauge tinplate No. 128 Illuminated Station and Terrace and additional street lights transform this scene when the room lights change the room from day to night on Richard Kughn's Lionel layout.

Robert Babas has installed lighting in all of the structures on his layout, as well as providing a variety of street lights and floodlights, and, of course, illuminated locomotive cabs and passenger car interiors.

A MODERN LIONEL LAYOUT

Lionel created its first dream book, the *Handbook for Model Builders*, in 1940. Included among the track plans (which were actually printed on blue paper with white lines like a construction blueprint) on page 71 was a massive model railroad that was noted as "an ideal project for a club." It included one freight yard and coach yard, complete with roundhouse and turntable on the lower level. The mainline pulled out of the terminal and ran in a reversing loop. The description goes on, saying "there are two grade approaches to the upper level, one from the lower level mainline and one from the yards . . . ."

The layout was designed to use exclusively 72-inch-diameter curves and switches. The plan filled a 10-foot, 8-inchx37-foot, 7-inch space. The plan is reproduced on page 151 of *The Lionel FasTrack Book*.

David Seebach built it even bigger than Lionel's artist could dream, bigger than Lionel's current showroom layout (see pages 210 and 211). Dave's empire is 12x42 feet. He enlarged the yards, added a few stub-ended sidings, and installed 39 switches. The bench work is constructed like an outdoor patio deck of 2x4s with half-inch plywood supporting the half-inch Homasote insulation board that is beneath the tracks. The track is all steel with extra wood ties and Woodland Scenic ballast. The scenery is paper toweling dipped in plaster and painted, then covered with ground foam for textures and covered with ready-built trees and bushes. The layout is powered by a Lionel Z transformer for switches and other constant voltage accessories. Three original Lionel ZW transformers and one modern ZW run the trains and other accessories.

Lionel's illustrations inspired hundreds of thousands of kids and adults to dream of a layout like this, and luckily Dave Seebach got to bring his dream to life.

David Seebach's Lionel layout has more than 500 square feet of scenery.

Dave added a pair of 15-foot-long sidings down the center of the layout to provide more storage and an intermodal yard with Lionel's Union Pacific Mi-Jack Intermodal Crane.

There are mountains and tunnels and, of course, rivers and bridges to be spanned with structures like Lionel's Trestle Bridge.

THE LIONEL VISITOR'S CENTER LAYOUT

One of the Lionel traditions is a display layout in its headquarters, now located in Mount Clemens, Michigan. There, at the Lionel Visitor's Center, you'll find a 12x30-foot layout that is periodically updated to include the newest operating accessories. However, the basic track work and scenery stay the same.

The layout uses standard track, but all of the curves (150 total) are 72 inches in diameter and all of the switches (16) are the matching O-72. The layout uses 140 pieces of 40-inch straight track. The upper level logging line is assembled from O-27 curves and straights. A second upper-level loop is assembled from American Flyer track.

The southeast, or mountain end, of the 12x30-foot Lionel Visitor's Center layout in Mount Clemens, Michigan, with the control panel just visible to the far left.

The southwest corner of the Lionel Visitor's Center layout with the logging railroad visible in the upper center.

LIONEL LARGE SCALE

Lionel's Large Scale 4-4-2 was an accurate 1/32 scale replica of a Pennsylvania Railroad class E-6 locomotive. Lionel's Large Scale trains run on two-rail track.

The massive stamped-steel Standard Gauge train toys of the early twentieth century embodied America's conception of what the best model railroad train should be: big, but not so big that you couldn't fit it into your lifestyle. That bit of toy train history was repeated in the 1980s when LGB began to export its series of expensive German-made toy trains.

The LGB products were costly because they were more than just rugged toys. The track was designed to be used outdoors, just like real railroad track. The cars and locomotives, while not completely weatherproof, were massive and sturdy enough spend the active part of their days running in whatever weather, including plowing snow off the tracks, their operators could tolerate.

LGB elected to re-create German narrow gauge trains because the relatively large locomotives and cars overhung the track, making them look like toys large enough to ride in. Narrow gauge was part of America's railroad history, too. The majority of the rails that reached the silver and gold veins in Colorado were laid with track that had rails three feet apart, rather than standard gauge of 4 feet, 8½ inches (in Germany, narrow gauge was established at one meter, about 39 inches).

In deciding to reproduce German narrow gauge, LGB noticed that in Germany in the 1920s and 1930s the massive Standard Gauge was considered the toy train to have, just as it was in America. So LGB selected the toy train Standard Gauge of 1¾ inches between the railheads.

LGB created accurate replicas of German locomotives and cars that operated on meter gauge track, making the cars and locomotives sized to match the 1¾-inch track gauge. The scale or proportion of the LGB models was about 22.5:1 or 1/22.5 scale. Later LGB offered replicas of both European and American cars and locomotives that were Standard Gauge, so the proportions of those models are close to 1/32 scale to match the track gauge (in 1/32 scale, Standard Gauge track would be about 1¾-inch gauge).

In 1987, Lionel introduced its first locomotive in Large Scale, an 0-4-0T (the "T" standing for the locomotive having the water and fuel carried on the locomotive in tanks, rather than in a separate tender). Lionel also offered a short flatcar, a very short passenger coach, and a replica of Reading Railroad four-wheel caboose in Large Scale, about 1/32 scale. Later Lionel produced an 0-6-0T 1880s-era locomotive and

Lionel offered this 1/32 scale GP7 in several paint schemes as part of the Large Scale series.

an eight-wheel caboose with baggage door that were styled to match narrow gauge prototypes of about 1/24 scale. Those locomotives and cars are still being produced today, usually decorated in bright Christmas colors.

In 1990, Lionel introduced a 1/32 scale replica of the Pennsylvania Railroad class E-6 Atlantic (which the company also offered in 1/48 scale Standard O), an Electro-Motive Corporation GP7 with a high short hood, a GP20 with a low short hood, a 40-foot sliding-door boxcar, and a plug-door reefer. Lionel also produced a 1/32 scale tank car, but it was

shortened about a third, so it looks far more toylike than the E-6, GP9, GP20, or the boxcar or reefer.

None of Lionel's products were designed to operate outdoors. The track has brass rails, and some of the track in the inexpensive Christmas sets is all plastic, which works just fine with the battery-powered versions of Lionel's 0-6-0T and 0-4-0T.

Apparently, Lionel viewed its Large Scale offerings as being the Standard Gauge of the 1990s, but its customers wanted the original stamped-steel stuff, so Lionel's Large Scale eventually morphed into a relatively inexpensive Christmas toy.

PART VII
THE NEW MILLENNIUM

The TrainMaster system of remote control allows you to operate up to 100 trains using this hand-held keypad. The locomotive is an SD90 MAC from the 2000 line.

B y the 1990s, the model railroad hobby had long demanded an easier method of running two or more trains at once than the traditional and complex "block" system of electrically isolated segments of track. To provide individual control for several trains without the use of blocks, Digital Command Control (DCC) was developed. DCC emerged in the late 1990s as the development of a dozen earlier systems, but it was created for two-rail direct current (DC). However, Lionel trains operated on three rails with alternating current (AC). In 1995, Lionel introduced its version of command control, dubbed TrainMaster Command Control, to operate the company's AC-powered locomotives and accessories.

TrainMaster Command Control allows you to operate two, three, or a dozen or more trains without the electrically isolating blocks. In fact, you can run a parade of trains, each just a foot or more from the caboose or observation

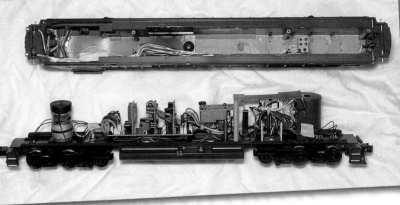

This Lionel replica of the General Electric Dash 8-32BWH is a true O scale model with TrainMaster Command Control, RailSounds, Odyssey System automatic speed control, directional lighting, ElectroCouplers, and fan-driven smoke.

car of the next, around any layout. That is the real thrill of TrainMaster Command Control: You are running trains, not controlling the track—which is precisely how a real railroad engineer runs his or her train.

The controller (called a CAB-1 Remote) for the TrainMaster system is a wireless remote, just a bit larger

"You know where we've been."

"Here's where we're going."

Lionel announced the TrainMaster control system in 1994 with a personal message from Richard Kughn, chairman and CEO of Lionel Trains, Inc.

than a typical television remote control. Since it has no wires, you can walk along beside your train or sit back in an easy chair and run the layout from the "tower." The CAB-1 Remote has a knob to control speed, a panic button (labeled "halt") to stop the trains, a reverse switch, a series of buttons to actuate RailSounds, and a set of numbered buttons so that you can dial up the number of each locomotive you want to control. You can also throw the track switches or operate action accessories from the buttons on the CAB-1 Remote. Locomotives and cars equipped with Lionel's ElectroCouplers can be uncoupled anywhere on the track at the push of a button. For conventional Lionel operating couplers, the handheld CAB-1 Remote can be used to actuate the FasTrack No. 6-12020 Uncoupling Track

or the No. 6-12054 Operating Track to uncouple cars or locomotives on these track sections (or to activate automatic cars that dump or have other animation).

Lionel's TrainMaster Command Control supplies a steady 18 volts to the rails; the speed control is inside the locomotive. The systems uses radio control to signal the receiver inside each TrainMaster-equipped locomotive to speed up, slow down, or reverse, and each of those functions is adjustable.

Lionel does not offer conversion kits for locomotives not factory-equipped with TMCC because the system is complex and very delicate to install. Lionel occasionally offers replacement freight trucks with the TrainMaster-actuated ElectroCouplers.

ALL THE BELLS AND WHISTLES

Back in 1935, Lionel was one of the first toy companies to understand the sales value of adding realistic sound to its air-powered whistle. In 1999, Lionel took another step with RailSounds, which uses digital recording to capture the exact sound of the whistles of each specific steam locomotive, the precise tones of the air horns that are unique to each brand of diesel, the sound of the bells that are used on even most modern diesels, and much more. RailSounds also reproduced the sound of air pumps, of air being released, and, later, of the engineers and a tower man talking to crews with CrewTalk Dialog and TowerCom announcements.

Digital reproduction is one of the earmarks of the new millennium, and Lionel is right there with best sound the company can find. You can ring the bells of modern diesels once or set them to sound continuously. The later Legacy Railroads system even allows to you adjust the response and instant quilling of real diesel horns.

Lionel has focused a lot of attention on getting the roar and rumble of real trains with RailSounds. The sound of the EMD diesels, for example, is different from those of General Electric's diesels, so Lionel has reproduced each of those sounds. Lionel's RailSounds also offers exact replicas of horns, brake applications, or steam locomotive startup or steam blow-off. And the chuffing of the steam locomotive or the growl of the diesel is synchronized to the speed of the model. It doesn't get any more realistic than that.

The RailSounds feature in Lionel's semi-scale replicas of the GE Dash 9-44W diesels in 2001 is a re-creation of the actual General Electric engine's, horns, and others sounds.

The RailSounds unit in the Standard O Lionel replica of the EMD Mac 90 has all the sounds of the full-size Electro-Motive Corporation's modern diesel.

LEGACY—GET THE FEEL OF IT

The RailSounds unit in the Standard O Lionel replica of the EMD Mac 90 has all the sounds of the full-size Electro-Motive Corporation's modern diesel.

Lionel introduced its Legacy Control System in 2007 with all of the controls on this Cab-2 Remote hand-held unit.

After introducing a system that could reproduce every imaginable real railroad locomotive, car, and structure sound, Lionel reproduced the massive feel of full-size railroading with the new Legacy control system.

Lionel launched the new Legacy control system in 2007. It re-creates the way a full-size locomotive reacts to throttle and brake controls. HO modelers have had momentum control as an option with digital command control for nearly 20 years. The upmarket digital command control systems (DCC, to HO modelers) have manual adjustments on their handheld throttles, so you can dial in more or less reaction time for the throttle and more or less coast-down time when the throttle is shut off. The Lionel Legacy system has these same options and more.

The Legacy system has 200 separate throttle stops for near-infinite speed variations and an adjustable horn control. Part of the "feel" that Legacy offers is the rumble and strain of a full-size locomotive trying get those hundreds of thousands of tons moving—the Legacy CAB-2 Remote handheld control actually vibrates as that power is put into play, and you can adjust level of vibration. You can select the locomotive you want to control with touch screen, and its name and number will appear on the LCD screen.

The Legacy remote controller is designed to be handheld and has a built-in rechargeable battery. The unit has a charger base that automatically recharges the battery with the CAB-2 Remote docked in its holder for a control panel–style unit. Lionel offers a Legacy Expansion Set so that you can gang two or more remote controllers and their charger bases together.

Like the TrainMaster system, you can also use the CAB-2 Remote controller to operate Lionel's ElectroCouplers anywhere on the layout. With some additional switch controllers on the layout, the CAB-2 Remote controller will operate the track switches. With accessory motor controllers for each accessory, the CAB-2 Remote can also be used operate Lionel's accessories like the coal loader or magnetic crane.

The Legacy system is designed to be capable of expanding as new technology develops. So in the future, you can expect computer interfacing for train control and dispatching functions and much, much more.

The Legacy Cab-2 Remote docks in this stand for automatic recharging.

Lionel's 2007 catalogs announced the latest in digital technology, Lionel's Legacy Control System.

FASTRACK

Lionel's FasTrack (left), like the modern Hudson, is far more realistic than the classic O-31 track or the postwar Hudson.

FasTrack, introduced in 2003, is one of the most successful products in Lionel's history because its appeal spreads across a wide range of Lionel enthusiasts. The track is easy enough to use that the casual operator likes it, and it is realistic enough the exact-scale "hi-rail" enthusiasts can use it.

Lionel introduced FasTrack as an easier and less-costly form of track for medium-priced train sets. By 2005, Lionel had expanded the FasTrack line to include three sizes of switches, four curve diameters, and a host of accessory pieces.

Lionel still offers traditional stamped-steel track. It has been part of the product line for over a century. However, any Lionel O Gauge or O-27 locomotive, freight car, or passenger car, from any time in that last century, will run just as well on FasTrack as on traditional Lionel track. With an adaptor track, you can even join FasTrack to traditional Lionel track on a single layout.

FasTrack has molded in plastic ties with realistic wood grain and simulated gray ballast that is designed to look exactly like loose grains of crushed rock. The FasTrack sections are joined by both plastic clips and metal rail joiners on the rails for maximum strength, perfect alignment, and reliable electrical conductivity. The FasTrack rails are shaped sheet metal for ample electrical current-carrying capacity and the strength to support the heaviest Lionel locomotive.

Vito Glimco operates this complex Lionel layout that was finished in just a few months, thanks to the simple FasTrack system.

Lionel advertised FasTrack, introduced in 2003, with an evocative painting reminiscent of its 1950s-era catalogs.

LIONEL'S FACTORY AND STORE

Lionel produced the first of the animated Lionel Midtown Hobby Shop buildings in 1999. The model has full interior lighting and a roof that is all skylights. Inside are three operational Lionel layouts, complete with scenery and bridges. On the shop's shelves and in its showcases are a host of Lionel products, as well as decorative flashing train signals. The 11 figures include both customers and the sales force. In 2003, Lionel offered a nearly identical building, but it was a Ford car dealership, with automobiles on rotating stands, salesmen, and buyers.

Lionel also offered a re-creation of the Lionel factory in 1999. The stamped-steel model was similar to the early Lionel Factory in Irvington, New Jersey. Inside, Lionel employees worked on assembling trains. The machinery and workers inside were static models, but the interior was fully painted and illuminated.

The 1993 Lionel No. 12767 Steam Clean & Wheel Grind Shop was actually three separate structures. A nozzle on the steam-cleaning tank sprayed smoke to simulate steam cleaning, the soft rollers rotated while lights flashed, and the wheel grinder generated sparks and sounds. The three modules, if placed end to end, were 37 inches long. This piece is sometimes considered to be the most interesting, and longest, of Lionel's accessories and ranks as one of Lionel's most spectacular models.

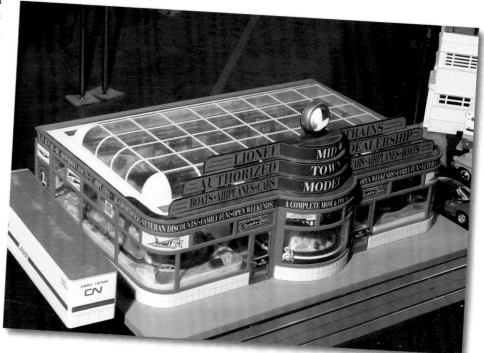

The Midtown Hobby Shop re-creates a massive Lionel train store.

There are three operating layouts, showcases full of models, and backup stock on the shelves inside the Lionel Midtown Hobby Shop.

The stamped-steel re-creation of the Lionel Factory was introduced in 1999.

The Steam Clean & Wheel Grind units were introduced in 1991, 1993, and 1995.

CARNIVAL TIME

Toy trains have a carnival atmosphere of their own, so it was only a matter of time before Lionel introduced replicas of carnival rides for its layouts. The series began in 2001 with both a 20-inch-tall Ferris wheel and a 9¾-inch-diameter carousel. Lionel has added another ride nearly every year since, including a huge swinging Viking ship (and, later, a pirate ship) ride, swinging chairs, the Scrambler (with double-rotating sets of seats), and a hot air balloon ride. Lionel has even re-created the carnival arcade midway with a series of animated accessories that include a shooting gallery, ring toss, test of strength, ball-toss, and cotton candy stall. In 2002, the operating lumberjacks appeared as the first in a continuing series of small platforms covered with simulated grass.

In 2003, the first of the playground series appeared. The Playtime Playground had a four-swing swing set, two teeter-totters, and a merry-go-round. Additional park scenes and playground centers are added each year.

Lionel's Scrambler ride, Carousel (in action), Duck Shooting Gallery, and Test O' Strength are a complete carnival scene on Lester Kuchner's layout in the Main Line Hobby store in East Norristown, Pennsylvania.

Lionel produced the Hot Air Balloon Ride to expand its carnival scene.

A giant swing adds even more fun to the carnival scene.

Lionel also has introduced a complete animated city park with the Mr. Spiff and Puddles and Playground Swings.

LIONEL'S GAS TURBINE

Alco produced the gas turbine for the Union Pacific in 1954, and Lionel has re-created it in both Standard O and HO scale.

Lionel produced a massive 21-inch-long Standard O 1/48 scale replica of the 1954 Union Pacific Alco Veranda (so called because there's a veranda-like walkway along the sides) Gas Turbine in 2001. The full-size locomotive was, essentially, two locomotives on one chassis, with a General Electric gas turbine driving the generator to deliver the power to 32 wheels. It was an odd combination of a very long diesel with a tender that would have looked appropriate behind any steam locomotive.

An 11½-inch-long HO scale version was offered in 2003. It was the fourth time Lionel ventured into the smaller scales. Lionel produced OO scale in 1937, HO scale in the 1960s and 1970s, and in 2004 it embarked on making a series of HO scale locomotives. When Lionel decided to produce an HO scale Veranda, it had already constructed a series of HO scale replicas of the Union Pacific 4-6-6-4 Challenger locomotives in 2003, again using the same research material the company had to produce its O scale versions a few years before.

The Lionel HO scale Alco Veranda Gas Turbine was very well detailed and operated smoothly, but it lacked the weight to pull the number of cars enthusiasts wanted it to. Lionel has a similar problem with Challenger, due in part to the tender weighing as much a half-dozen freight cars. Eventually, Lionel went back to what it knows best, creating superb O Gauge and Standard O models.

The Lionel models of Veranda gas turbine included an engineer, fireman, and panel details.

Lionel's HO model of the Alco gas turbine was as highly detailed as its Standard O version.

Lionel tried small scale again in 2003 and 2004 with a series of 4-6-6-4 Challenger steam locomotives and a replica of the Union Pacific Veranda Gas Turbine as advertised in the February 2004 issue of *Railmodel Journal*.

THOMAS AND FRIENDS

Thomas the Tank is working his way around a simple 4x8-foot oval built by Michael Ulewicz for his grandchildren.

Lionel has never lost sight of its need to spark children's interest in its products. Every Lionel train set has built-in play value, beyond simply running a train around the track. The trains can reverse, horns and whistle can sound, and cars can be coupled even in the lowest-priced sets. And Lionel provides several add-on products, with an endless array of action cars and accessories. First, though, Lionel has to grab the children's attention. It did that in the early 1990s with *Thomas and Friends*–themed toys. In an age where probably only one child in a hundred has ridden on a train, but where nearly every child watches television, Lionel decided to use the popularity of the *Thomas and Friends* series to generate interest in model trains.

In fact, the *Thomas and Friends* episodes are actually filmed on a huge model railroad. The trains are about the same size as Lionel's Large Scale. The locomotives and some foe cars have animated faces, and they all talk. The series is filmed in England, so the trains are all British proto-types. Lionel had its first Large Scale Thomas, with coaches Clarabelle and Annie, in 1993.

Lionel has produced replicas of the Thomas the Tank locomotives and cars in both O and Large Scale. Lionel did

Lionel produces both Large Scale and O scale recreations of Thomas the Tank.

not animate the locomotive fronts, but most include four different interchangeable faces: happy, surprised, sad, and angry. The star of the show is Thomas, of course, but Percy, James, Diesel, Iron 'Ary, and Iron Bert all have roles in various episodes. Lionel offers them all in O Gauge, too.

Lionel also offers the talking passenger cars Clarabelle and Annie, the two Troublesome Trucks gondolas, a flatcar with Harold the Helicopter, the dirty ballast hopper S. C. Ruffy, and a version of the Lionel Automatic Gateman where Sir Topham Hatt pops out of the shed every time the train passes.

PART VIII

THE REAL RAILROADS

LIONEL'S REAL RAILROADS

The Virginian has a romantic sound to it, and the rear railroad was spectacular with an electrified mainline over the Appalachians using locomotives similar to Lionel's replica of the EP-5.

Over the last 100-plus years, Lionel has produced replicas of at least one locomotive or freight car for virtually every significant real railroad in America. In the 1940s, Lionel focused on creating replicas of locomotives that would appeal to specific geographic segments of the country, with New York Central and Pennsylvania Railroad models for the East, the Milwaukee and Union Pacific for the Midwest, and the Santa Fe for the West. Later Lionel created a more diverse assortment of road names for both locomotives and cars.

Generally, each real railroad's steam locomotives had a style, with minor differences in shapes unique to that specific railroad. However, when the diesels appeared, dozens of real railroads bought the same locomotive, so Lionel merely had to create new paint schemes for these. Still, Lionel has

The Soo Line, from the upper Midwest, has bright red-and-white paint schemes that Lionel has duplicated on this Traditional model of the EMD GP38-2 from 1993. Here it is operating on the Milwaukee Model Railroad Club's layout.

Lionel produced an extended-vision caboose and two-bay ACF Centerflow covered hopper for the Soo fans in 1993.

been amazingly consistent in matching the correct paint schemes to correct locomotives.

Electric locomotives, however, were only purchased by a limited number of real railroads. The Pennsylvania Railroad was the sole customer for the GG1, although the locomotives lasted so long they were painted in a variety of colors, including Conrail and Amtrak schemes. The GG1 has been one of Lionel's best-selling locomotives for over 50 years.

Lionel wanted another electric locomotive that might sell as well as its legendary GG1, so in the 1950s the company opted for the New Haven E-33 (which was also offered in reasonably authentic Virginian and Conrail schemes). Lionel's third electric is a semi-scale replica of the General Electric double-ended EP-5 electric that was made only for the New Haven, but Lionel painted it to match vaguely similar Pennsylvania and Great Northern and Milwaukee Road double-ended electrics.

The real railroads' widespread use of single diesel models has made it possible for Lionel to offer replicas of locomotives from every Class 1 railroad and from dozens of smaller roads, as well. Sometimes the paint scheme has been selected for its impact value, like the gold-and-black Monon diesels, or the most unusual painted steam locomotives like the maroon Chicago & Alton Railroad versions or the bright blue New Jersey Central's. Other selections have been made to target locomotives for specific geographic areas like those from the

Lionel has re-created a few locomotives for the Midwestern Monon Railroad, including this semi-scale replica of the Alco C420 on Mike Raschig's layout.

following railroads: the Gulf, Mobile & Ohio, the Minneapolis & St. Louis, the Florida East Coast, the Toledo Peoria & Western, the Alaska Railroad, or the Mexico's Ferromex (as a replica of its EMD SD70ACE locomotive in 2008).

THE SANTA FE RAILWAY

It is ironic that, nationally, more people today recognize the Lionel orange-and-blue logo than recognize the logo of any real railroad, except perhaps Amtrak. However, within certain geographic areas, the major railroads do have recognizable logos or, as the railroads called them, heralds. That railroad herald recognition diminished considerably when people stopped riding trains.

During the first 60 years of the last century, when Lionel was growing tremendously, part of that growth stemmed from some very clever marketing including, of course, producing models with heralds and paint schemes of the real railroads in the major population centers.

Lionel's early growth centered in the major metropolitan areas in the Northeast Corridor and along the Great Lakes to Chicago. As such, the toy maker picked Pennsylvania and New York Central Railroad prototypes for its models. After World War II, though, Lionel's business expanded more into the Midwest and West, and concurrently, the nation's awareness of railroads other than their local mainlines increased.

The Santa Fe Railway ran from Chicago to Los Angeles at the time, and in 1948 the Santa Fe silver, red, and yellow warbonnet passenger diesels were probably recognized by more Americans than Lionel's logo. Lionel, of course, knew that and proceeded to offer a continuing series of locomotives, freight cars, and passenger cars painted in the Santa Fe Railway's colors and markings. Lionel's first diesel, the magnificent replica of the ElectroMotive Division of General Motors' F3A, was introduced in 1948 in the Santa Fe's silver, red, and yellow warbonnet scheme. Since then, many more variations of this model have been made. Significantly, Lionel's F3A was also offered in New York Central's two-tone gray to be sure Lionel's core eastern market did not feel neglected.

Lionel has introduced replicas of the most modern diesels over the past 50 years, including models that displayed the Santa Fe's early black-and-silver freight diesels, the later blue-with-yellow-markings diesels, and the latest BNSF merger paint schemes. Lionel even offered a replica of the Santa Fe's unique steel caboose from the 1940s.

To find out more about the Santa Fe Railway, visit the Santa Fe Railway Historical & Modeling Society's website at www.atsfrr.net.

The Lionel FA-1 and FB-1 (left) became the diesels used on most of Lionel's entry-level train sets. Ralph Johnson's F-3A (right) in Wabash colors is a rare one from 1955.

Lionel's first diesels were these replicas of the Santa Fe F3A and F3B diesels. The extruded-aluminum cars arrived in 1952 to complete this *Super Chief* re-creation on Gene Szymanowski's layout.

NEW YORK CENTRAL

The New York Central Railroad, like the Pennsylvania, Santa Fe, New Haven, Rio Grande, and others, is long gone, merged into a series of conglomerate railroads. First, the New York Central merged with the Pennsylvania to become the short-lived Penn-Central Railroad, now part of Conrail. Not surprisingly, Lionel has offered locomotives for all of these, but the 'Central was one of Lionel's first choices for its early twentieth-century Standard Gauge and O Gauge electric locomotives back in 1924. And it was the New York Central that provided the prototype for Lionel's famous Scale Hudson in 1937, as well as the paint scheme for Lionel's first diesel, the F3A, in 1950.

Lionel has generally been meticulous in decorating its diesel locomotives only for real railroads that actually owned that particular version. If the New York Central had them, Lionel usually re-created models—from the replicas of the EMD F3A and the FT cab diesels to the sleek Alco FA-2 and PA-1 diesels and replicas of NYC electrics.

One of Lionel's most artistic renditions was its re-creation of the streamlined version of the New York Central Hudson. The New York Central Hudson had a bullet-draped nose, rounded extensions to the tops and bottoms of tender, and added skirts below the running boards. All were part of a

The exact-scale New York Central Dreyfus 4-6-4 Hudson is 24 inches long.

streamlined design by Henry Dreyfus; thus these locomotives became known as the Dreyfus Hudsons. Lionel has also produced simulations of the Dreyfus Hudson as 14-inch-long toys since 1946, but a 24-inch-long accurate-scale replica appeared in 2002, and again in 2008.

A New York Central work train on Gil Bruck's layout. The locomotive is actually a Pennsylvania Railroad prototype that Lionel lettered New York Central in 1985.

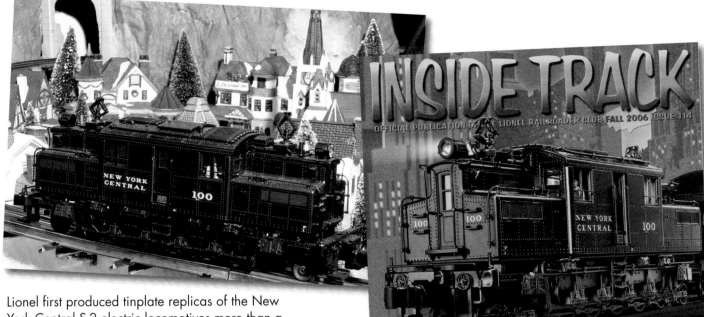

Lionel first produced tinplate replicas of the New York Central S-2 electric locomotives more than a hundred years ago. In 2006, Lionel brought this locomotive back as an exact-scale model.

A large proportion of the locomotives Lionel produces are eventually offered in the striking two-tone gray paint schemes of the New York Central, including the Fairbanks-Morse H16-44; the EMD F3A, F3B, E7A, and E7B; the Alco RF-16 and RS-11; and the Alco FA-2 (both in O-27 and exact scale). Lionel has even offered the modern-era EMD SD80MAC diesel with Amtrak hi-level passenger cars in New York Central two-tone gray.

To find more about the New York Central system, visit its historical society's website at www.nycshs.org. The Conrail Historical Society's website is www.thecrhs.org.

Lionel featured the new S-2 electric locomotive (with third rail shoes in place on the trucks) on the cover of the Fall 2006 issue of *Inside Track* magazine.

The EMD F3A and F3B have been Lionel's most popular diesels since their introduction in the 1950s. This is the 1990s New York Central model.

THE PENNSYLVANIA
RAILROAD

Lionel produces very limited runs of some striking-looking locomotives, like this Pennsylvania Railroad class T-1 6-4-4-6 articulated, that are instant collectors' items.

Lionel introduced its replica of the General Electric class EP-5 electric locomotive in 1958 to match the Pennsylvania Railroad's Tuscan Red passenger paint scheme.

For Lionel's first 50 years, its customers only wanted toy trains that looked something like the real thing—exact scale and super details would not arrive until 1940, and then only on a very few Lionel models. In selecting Pennsylvania Railroad locomotives for its toy trains, Lionel achieved instant product recognition because many of Lionel's customers had been passengers on trains pulled by those Pennsylvania locomotives. In fact, the railroad's reputation as "The Standard Railroad of the World" was part of the reason Lionel's second exact-scale locomotive was a replica of the Pennsylvania's 0-6-0 class A-6 switcher that worked the freight yards.

When Lionel resumed production after World War II, its headline steam locomotive was a much-compressed replica of the 6-8-6 steam turbine locomotive (see page 120). Then in 1947, Lionel's first postwar electric locomotive was a replica of the GG1 (see page 133)—both locomotives were only operated by the Pennsylvania Railroad. Later, Lionel offered diesels in the Penn Central paint scheme that resulted from the Pennsylvania and New York Central Railroads merging, and Lionel has re-created the diesels from today in Conrail colors.

The Pennsylvania Railroad Technical & Historical Society's website can be found at www.prrths.com, and the Conrail Historical Society website is www.thecrhs.org.

Lionel offered replicas of the small Pennsylvania Railroad class B6, its first postwar switcher, in 1955. It was reintroduced in 1975 and reintroduced in the 1990s. The *Polar Express* appeared in 2004 with a relettered Nickel Plate Railroad 2-8-4 Berkshire, a match for the locomotive in the motion picture.

THE UNION PACIFIC RAILROAD

The Union Pacific Railroad caught America's attention in 1934 with its brand-new articulated *M10000*. Lionel offered its replica of the yellow-and-brown *M10000* in 1934 as its first streamliner (see pages 78 and 79). Lionel did not offer another Union Pacific locomotive until 1950 with its replicas of the Alco FA-2 diesels (see pages 134 and 135).

The Union Pacific became a dream railroad for model railroaders in the 1940s when it ordered one of the largest steam locomotives ever produced: the articulated 4-8-8-4 Big Boy. The locomotive was far too long to operate on Lionel's tight curves, but in 2001, Lionel created the slightly smaller version as part of its LionMaster series (see pages 178 and 179). It would squeeze around 31-inch curves. In 1999, Lionel offered a near-scale Big Boy, but it would only negotiate 72-inch curves.

Over the past 50 years, the Union Pacific has been one of the more common railroads in the Lionel catalog. Lionel has produced replicas of nearly every type of diesel the Union Pacific operated. One of the most popular Lionel steam locomotives is its re-creation of the Union Pacific 2-8-0 Consolidation.

The Union Pacific Historical Society website can be found at www.uphs.org.

Lionel's replica of the E7A and E7B diesels that pulled the Union Pacific's *City of Los Angeles* and *City of San Francisco* streamliners.

The Union Pacific 4-6-6-4 articulated Challenger on Robert Babas' layout is one of the larger Lionel O scale steam locomotives.

Lionel introduced its first exact-scale 2-8-0 Consolidation in 2000. The model is a replica of the Union Pacific and Southern Pacific's locomotives, including the round Vanderbilt tender.

Lionel is reproducing the largest steam and diesel locomotives, including modern machines like the Burlington Northern EMD SD70MAC and Union Pacific General Electric Dash 9-44CW.

THE MILWAUKEE ROAD

Gil Bruck has a collection of Lionel's Milwaukee Road diesels that include this lash up of two GP7s with two different Milwaukee Road paint schemes and an SD18.

Few Americans have even heard of the Milwaukee Road, which was acquired by the Soo Line in 1986. Despite the road's anonymity, Lionel has re-created almost as many Milwaukee Road locomotives and passenger cars as it has for Pennsylvania or Santa Fe. Why? No one knows for sure, but it could be that the orange-and-black paint on the Milwaukee's diesel and electric locomotives looks about as close as you could get to what Lionel might have picked for its own diesels' colors (Lionel has produced its own diesels, but they are blue with orange stripes).

One of Lionel's first streamlined passenger trains was its 1937 Milwaukee Road *Hiawatha* that utilized the articulated cars from the Union Pacific *M10000* but in Milwaukee orange and black. Lionel produced an exact-scale *Hiawatha* in 2006 (see pages 80 to 81) and a stamped-steel Standard Gauge version in 2001.

One of Lionel's first Standard Gauge locomotives was a very much foreshortened 0-4-0 model of the massive Bipolar (which at full size had a 2-4-4-4-4-4-2 wheel arrangement). In 1928, Lionel offered a much larger Standard Gauge version with a 4-4-4 wheel arrangement. It was almost 19 inches long, the largest electric locomotive Lionel produced. However, it had roughly half the number of wheels and was proportionally shorter length. In 2007, however, Lionel created exact-scale replicas of the massive Milwaukee Road class EP-2 Bipolar electric that in the relatively smaller (compared to Lionel's Standard Gauge) O scale is 20 inches long.

The Milwaukee had a newer series of massive electric locomotives called Little Joes, which had 12 axles and double-ended noses similar the EMD F3A. Lionel painted its model of the General Electric EP-5 four-axle electric (the same model as the New Haven electric on page 246) in Milwaukee Road orange and black to serve as a caricature of the Little Joe.

Lionel has also painted nearly all of its diesels in Milwaukee Road orange and black, and it offered several steam locomotives and variety of freight cars and cabooses in Milwaukee colors.

To find out more about the Milwaukee Road, visit its historical association's website at www.mrha.com.

Lionel crammed a pair of six-wheel trucks beneath a GP20 body to create a caricature of the much longer EMD SD28 diesel.

Lionel offered its replica of Fairbanks-Morse H16-44 diesel to match a Milwaukee prototype in 2001.

THE NEW HAVEN RAILROAD

Lionel produced the F3A and F3B in the unusual checkerboard New Haven paint scheme in 1978.

If you live in California or Kansas or Oregon, you may never have heard of New Haven as anything more than a city in Connecticut. The New York, New Haven & Hartford (NYNH&H) railroad was primarily a commuter and freight line serving just four states: Connecticut, New York, Rhode Island, and Massachusetts. The New Haven merged into Penn-Central in 1969. After Penn-Central's 1976 bankruptcy, much at the former New Haven was trasnferred to Amtrak.

In 1956, Lionel produced the first of several replicas of one of the most famous New Haven electric locomotives, the General Electric EP-5, in the bright orange, black, and white paint scheme. The model, like the prototype, had pantographs on both ends. Lionel's model, however, is considerably shorter than the prototype, which had six-wheel trucks on each end.

Lionel also offered the E-33 electric locomotive that was built for the Virginian Railroad in New Haven orange, black, and white and the same locomotive in Conrail blue and white.

In 1958, Lionel offered the EMD F3A and F3B diesel in the New Haven silver, white, red, and black paint scheme and the New Haven's Alco PA-1 and PB-1 in 1999. Lionel also has offered a bay window caboose in New Haven paint, but it is the electric locomotives that are Lionel's most significant New Haven replicas.

The New Haven Railroad Historical Society website is www.nhrhta.org/ and the Conrail Historical Society website is www.thecrhs.org.

Lionel offered the Alco PA-1 and PB-1 in 1999 painted for the Pennsylvania Railroad and, later, in New Haven paint.

THE BURLINGTON NORTHERN RAILROAD

The Burlington in the Burlington Northern Railroad was originally the Chicago, Burlington & Quincy Railroad. In 1970, the Burlington merged with the Northern Pacific, the Spokane, Portland & Seattle, and the Great Northern railroads to form the Burlington Northern. The BN disappeared in 1996 with the merger of the Santa Fe and Burlington Northern into BNSF (Burlington Northern Santa Fe).

Lionel has produced locomotives and freight cars for most of these railroads (except for the SP&S). Many serious model railroaders consider 1970 to be the best year in the history of railroads because all of the Burlington Northern's subsidiary roads still had their colorful diesel colors with just new BN numbers. By collecting these, you have gone back in time to a specific time and place.

To find out more about the history of these railroads, visit the following websites: www.burlingtonroute.com (the Burlington Route Historical Society), www.gnrhs.org (the Great Northern Railway Historical Society), www.nprha.org/ (the Northern Pacific Railway Historical Association), www.spshs. org/ (the Spokane, Portland & Seattle Historical Society), and www.fobnr.org (the Friends of the Burlington Northern).

Lionel produces replicas of the most modern diesels like this O Scale EMD SD70MAC in a short-lived BNSF Executive paint scheme.

Lionel offers enough different paint schemes to allow you to recreate a solid Burlington Northern train. Lionel has offered dozens of replicas of Burlington Northern equipment, including this Standard O 40-foot semi-scale boxcar, 40-foot Hi-Cube boxcar, four-bay covered hopper, and extended-vision caboose.

THE RIO GRANDE RAILROAD

In the 1990s, Lionel fans finally got the Alco PA-1 and PB-1 they had been asking for over the past five decades.

The Rio Grande Railroad has become the symbol of mountain railroading. Dozens of Western films have been shot along the remaining tracks of the now tourist-only narrow gauge Rio Grande Railroad in Southwestern Colorado.

Narrow gauge lines like the Rio Grande's were built with rails spaced three feet from railhead to railhead while the standard gauge railroads were 4 feet, 8½ inches from railhead to railhead. The narrow gauge cars and loco-motives were also about three-fourths the size of standard gauge, which meant the bridges could be lighter, tunnels smaller, and construc-tion generally less costly. The narrow gauge lines were abandoned by the late 1940s, but the standard gauge Rio Grande mainline from Denver to Salt Lake City is still active. The Rio Grande merged into the Union Pacific (along with the Southern Pacific, Western Pacific, and Missouri Pacific) in 1982. Lionel has offered diesels for all these roads.

Lionel has produced a few Large Scale models lettered for the Rio Grande narrow gauge (see page 212 and 213), but the majority of Lionel's Rio Grande models are re-creations of the standard gauge diesels and cabooses of the last 30 years.

To learn more about the Denver & Rio Grande Railroad, visit the following website: www.drgw.org.

The new Lionel Standard O caboose to match the shape of the Santa Fe cabooses of the 1940s, but painted and lettered for roads like the Grande.

Larry LaJambe has selected a variety of Lionel replicas of Rio Grande locomotives for his spectacular layout, including this Alco RS-3 (lower right) and EMD SD45 (lower left).

AMTRAK TRAINS

Lionel has re-created an O Scale replica of the General Electric Dash 8-32BWH used by Amtrak.

Lionel has always offered replicas of whatever was the latest and newest in real railroad equipment, so you can expect that the company would supply its fans with replicas of the latest Amtrak equipment, too.

Amtrak was created in 1971, and soon after the deal was done, the cars and locomotives that were absorbed into Amtrak from railroads across America were repainted.

Lionel first offered the EMD F3A (Amtrak did not operate F3A units, but it did have the much longer 12-wheeled E9 diesels) in 1972, and Lionel also offered the FA-2 (which Amtrak did not operate) in 1976. When Lionel released more modern replicas of these, they were offered in Amtrak colors. Lionel also eventually offered the massive 12-wheeled EMD Dash 9 (No. 510) in 1999 and the 8-wheeled Dash 8 (No. 809) in 2002.

Lionel also offered its smallest smooth-side passenger cars, including the dome car, painted for Amtrak in 1976. In 2002, Lionel introduced near-scale 18-inch replicas of the Amtrak Superliner double-deck cars.

In 2005, Lionel introduced its replica of the Acela trains that travel the Northeast Corridor's commuter line. The three-car train and locomotive was a Lionel breakthrough in 2005. The train included a bistro car and two business-class coaches with full interiors and about a dozen passengers in each car. The model even included a re-creation of the prototype's tilting mechanism to tilt the cars at speeds over 25 scale miles per hour. The car doors automatically open, and the step lights are illuminated when the train stops. The cars are close-coupled, so the train needs a 72-inch minimum-diameter curve.

The Amtrak Historical Society website is www.amtrak-historicalsociety.com.

Lionel has offered a variety of the extruded-aluminum reproductions of real corrugated-steel side passenger cars. These are the Amtrak Vista Dome and the Amtrak Full Dome on the Lionel Visitor's Center layout.

Lionel offered its O-27 semi-scale F3A and F3B diesels in Baltimore & Ohio markings in 1956 and in 1972 in the Amtrak arrow markings, like on these units on Ralph Johnson's layout.

Lionel produced an incredible replica of the Acela commuter train in 2005, which includes an operating banking feature when the train goes through curves.

LIONEL'S MODERN MOVIE STAR TRAINS

Lionel's O Gauge replica of the *Hogwarts Express* has an accurate British whistle sound and puffing smoke.

Perhaps history does repeat itself. Today, Lionel offers massive models about the size of the Standard Gauge Lionel trains that were so coveted by the children in the 1920s and 1930s. While today's children have never heard of the New York Central or the *Blue Comet*, they do know all about *The Polar Express* that Lionel introduced in 2004 and the *Hogwarts Express* that Lionel has offered since in 2007.

Lionel had its O Gauge version of *The Polar Express* in the shops the day the movie hit the big screens and Harry Potter's *Hogwarts Express* when the third movie was first

The locomotive and cars on Lionel's *Hogwarts Express* are replicas of the train used in the motion picture.

Lionel has re-created the *Polar Express* as part of its relatively low-cost O-27 series.

playing. Lionel also has massive Large Scale replicas of both of these motion picture stars. Lionel made *The Polar Express* and *Hogwarts Express* essential parts of the Christmas scene in thousands of homes.

The 2-8-2 Mikado that Lionel created to head its 2008 Large Scale *Polar Express* is somewhat foreshortened, but it still one of the largest models Lionel has produced. The 4-6-0

that pulls the 2007 *Hogwarts Express* is also a massive model. These G Gauge replicas are made primarily from injection-molded plastic, including the track and rails. No, there is not the heft of stamped steel of Lionel's 1930s-era Standard Gauge models, but both *The Polar Express* and *Hogwarts Express* are truly low-priced trains, powered by batteries. In today's dollars, you could not buy even one of those fabled Standard Gauge stamped-steel freight cars from the 1930s for the price of the entire *Polar Express* or *Hogwarts Express* train set.

Lionel certainly did not forget the three-rail electric train market with these movie trains. Both *The Polar Express* and *Hogwarts Express* are available as O Gauge replicas. The locomotive used to film *The Polar Express* was a repainted full-size restored Pere Marquette Railroad 2-8-4 Berkshire No. 1225. Lionel actually has an exact-scale version of No. 1225 in the Standard O series, but you could buy four complete Polar Express train sets for the price of Lionel's Standard O Pere Marquette Berkshire. If you could afford it, Lionel even offered a Standard O replica of the C & O Allegheny tender along with Legacy RailSounds to upgrade your Traditional O version of *The Polar Express* (again, the tender itself is half the price of the entire *Polar Express* train set).

The Polar Express passing through scenery on Gino Szymanowski's layout.

Lionel's replica of *The Polar Express* train was designed to sell at the lowest possible price, so it has a somewhat foreshortened 2-8-4 Berkshire locomotive and passenger cars. The *Hogwarts Express* is also a semi-scale model with locomotive the correct size and only slightly foreshortened coaches. The O Gauge replicas operate on modern FasTrack and are powered and controlled like all of Lionel's trains.

The O Gauge replicas of *The Polar Express* and *Hogwarts Express* train sets are nearly three times the price of the massive Large Scale Lionel replicas, so Mom and Dad have the choice of an heirloom that is rugged enough to last through generations or a larger modern toy train. Again, Lionel has used its history of expertise in the toy market to produce train sets that are both highly desirable and affordable to yet another generation of children (and their parents).

INDEX